KU-722-616

BEST OF
Lisbon

Terry Carter & Laura Dunston

Colour-Coding & Maps

Each chapter has a colour code along the banner at the top of the page, which is also used for text and symbols on maps (eg all venues reviewed in the Highlights chapter are orange on the maps). The fold-out maps inside the front and back covers are numbered from 1 to 6. All sights and venues in the text have map references; eg (4, E2) means Map 4, grid reference E2. See p96 for map symbols.

Prices

Multiple prices listed with reviews (eg €10/5) usually indicate adult/concession admission to a venue. Concession prices can include senior, student, member or coupon discounts. Meal cost and room rate categories are listed at the start of the Eating and Sleeping chapters, respectively.

Text Symbols

- ☎ telephone
- ✉ address
- 🖥 email/website address
- € admission
- 🕑 opening hours
- ⓘ information
- Ⓜ metro
- 🚌 bus
- Ⓟ parking available
- ♿ wheelchair access
- ✗ on-site/nearby eatery
- ♣ child-friendly venue
- Ⓥ good vegetarian selection
- ❄ air-con
- ✗ nonsmoking

Best of Lisbon
1st edition – May 2006

Published by Lonely Planet Publications Pty Ltd
ABN 36 005 607 983

Australia Head Office, Locked Bag 1, Footscray, Vic 3011
☎ 03 8379 8000, fax 03 8379 8111
🖥 talk2us@lonelyplanet.com.au

USA 150 Linden St, Oakland, CA 94607
☎ 510 893 8555, toll free 800 275 8555
fax 510 893 8572
🖥 info@lonelyplanet.com

UK 72–82 Rosebery Ave, Clerkenwell, London
EC1R 4RW
☎ 020 7841 9000, fax 020 7841 9001
🖥 go@lonelyplanet.co.uk

This title was commissioned in Lonely Planet's London office and produced by: **Commissioning Editor** Sally Schafer **Coordinating Editors** Victoria Harrison, Sarah Hassall **Coordinating Cartographer** Emma McNicol **Layout Designer** Jacqueline Mcleod **Cartographers** Natasha Velleley, Diana Duggan **Managing Cartographer** Mark Griffiths **Cover Designer** Marika Kozak **Project Managers** Chris Love, Eoin Dunlevy **Mapping Development** Paul Piaia **Desktop Publishing Support** Mark Germanchis **Thanks to** Wendy Wright, Brendan Dempsey, Adriana Mammarella, Celia Wood, Sally Darmody, Michala Green, Stefanie Di Trocchio, Fiona Siseman, Glenn Beanland.

Photographs by Lonely Planet Images and Greg Elms except for the following: p7 Esbin Anderson; p78 Jeffrey Becom; p8, p12, p36 Anders Blomqvist; p5 Martin Lladó; p33, p75 Martin Moos; p74 Damien Simonis; p56, p78 Oliver Strewe; p60 Wayne Walton; p6, p62 Julia Wilkinson. **Cover photograph** Ascensor da Gloria Lisbon Portugal, Cro Magnon/Alamy. All images are copyright of the photographers unless otherwise indicated. Many of the images in this guide are available for licensing from Lonely Planet Images: www.lonelyplanetimages.com.

ISBN 1 74104 088 4

Printed through Colorcraft Ltd, Hong Kong.

Printed in China

Acknowledgments Metropolitano de Lisboa Network Diagram © January 2006 Metropolitano de Lisboa, E.P.

Contents

From the Publisher

THE AUTHORS
Terry Carter

Terry left Sydney seven years ago after toiling far too long in Sydney's publishing industry. Having erroneously concluded that travel writing was a far more glamorous occupation than designing books or websites, he has now been travel writing for several years and has travelled extensively through Europe and the Middle East, where until recently he was based. Lisbon was one of the first places Terry visited after moving from Australia and his fondness for the city hasn't dimmed since that first visit. Terry has a master's degree in media studies and divides his time between freelance travel writing, photography and web design.

Lara Dunston

Lara has degrees in film, communications, international studies and screenwriting, and a career that's embraced writing, filmmaking, media education and now travel writing – motivated by journeys to 50 countries. Lara first saw Lisbon in the film *Foreign Land,* while in Brazil researching her master's degree in Latin American cinema. When she first visited Portugal in the '90s she discovered the melancholy city of the movie. While the Lisbon of the new millennium is modern and optimistic, and she loves the *bravura* of the Bairro Alto, Lara has a soft spot for the romance and nostalgia of old-world Lisbon.

LONELY PLANET AUTHORS

Why is our travel information the best in the world? It's simple: our authors are independent, dedicated travellers. They don't research using just the Internet or phone, and they don't take freebies in exchange for positive coverage. They travel widely, to all the popular spots and off the beaten track. They personally visit thousands of hotels, restaurants, cafés, bars, galleries, palaces, museums and more – and they take pride in getting all the details right, and telling it how it is. For more, see the authors section on **www.lonelyplanet.com**.

PHOTOGRAPHER
Greg Elms

Greg Elms has contributed to Lonely Planet for over 15 years, and has completed numerous commissions in that time, including five books in the World Food series. In Lisbon he had some 140 locations to cover in eight days, which required constant refuelling at various cafés with the local Portuguese tarts. The local tipple *ginjinha,* served at small bars around town, provided much-needed liquid refreshment. Greg was ably assisted in navigating this labyrinthine city by the friendly folk at Tourism Lisboa. Eventually settling down to a freelance career in Melbourne, he now works regularly for many outlets, and, of course, book publishers such as Lonely Planet.

SEND US YOUR FEEDBACK

We love to hear from travellers – your comments keep us on our toes and help make our books better. Our well-travelled team reads every word on what you loved or loathed about this book. Although we cannot reply individually to postal submissions, we always guarantee that your feedback goes straight to the appropriate authors, in time for the next edition – and the most useful submissions are rewarded with a free book. To send us your updates – and find out about Lonely Planet events, newsletters and travel news – visit our award-winning website: **www.lonelyplanet.com/feedback**.

Note: we may edit, reproduce and incorporate your comments in Lonely Planet products such as guidebooks, websites and digital products, so let us know if you don't want your comments reproduced or your name acknowledged. For a copy of our privacy policy visit **www.lonelyplanet.com/privacy**.

Introducing Lisbon

Part raucous port town, part elegant Western European city, Lisbon (Lisboa) is a city with a unique ambience. The Portuguese capital is aesthetically astonishing, a roller-coaster ride of seven hills that have innumerable beautiful vistas and breathtaking historical sights, with the Rio Tejo (Tagus River) a constant reminder of Lisbon's past seafaring glories.

Lisbon's city centre is a tiny time capsule from the 1800s, with its perfectly aligned cobblestone streets and centuries-old shops selling hats, gloves, port and *bacalhau* (dried, salted cod), amid the smell of roasting chestnuts from the street stalls. Order is forgotten, though, when you take one of Lisbon's endearingly faded yellow trams up the hills either side of the city. Alfama, with its labyrinthine, tipsy streets of *fado* (melancholic folk song) music and faded bars,

awaits on one side; and on the other the is Bairro Alto, famous for its bar scene, where patrons clutching *caipirinhas* (a cocktail made with the Brazilian rum–like spirit, Cachaça, limes, sugar and ice) spill out onto the atmospheric streets. Down by the Rio Tejo, a different scene is played out as seafood restaurants present the daily catch, and Lisbon's club scene gets ready for action that doesn't finish until the sun rises.

While you might get the impression that Lisbon is merely a very elegant museum exhibit, its new hotels and restaurants are turning well-travelled heads. Lisbon is simply a city that protects its past and considers the future very carefully. Once you have visited, you'll probably agree that this is a wise move.

Lisbon favourites: yellow trams and Sé Cathedral (p9)

Neighbourhoods

Lisbon sits on the north bank of the Rio Tejo (Tagus River), 15km from the Atlantic Ocean, nestling beautifully among seven small hills – São Jorge, Estréla, Santa Catarina, São Pedro de Alcântara, Graça, Senhora do Monte, and Penha de França – each with *miradouros* (vantage points) that offer wonderful views of the city and the Rio Tejo.

Baixa's grid of bustling black-and-white tiled streets is Lisbon's historic heart, and the pedestrianised Rua Augusta its commercial centre, with excellent shopping and outdoor cafés. To the south, Baixa extends to the grand waterfront gateway of Praça do Comércio. To the east is Lisbon's famous castle, Castelo de São Jorge, accessible by a walk through the ancient maze-like streets of **Alfama**. Further on from here is charming, working-class **Graça**.

To the west of Baixa is the elegant **Chiado** shopping area and then the bohemian **Bairro Alto**, with hip shops and buzzy bars lining its steep narrow streets. Further on again are the embassies and mansions of leafy 18th-century **Lapa**.

To the north of Baixa are the lively squares of Praça da Figueira and Praça de Dom Pedro IV (Rossio). From here, Rua da Palma heads north, becoming Avenida Almirante Reis on its 6-km run to the airport. From Praça dos Restauradores the elegant boulevard of Avenida da Liberdade heads northwest to Praça Marquês de Pombal and Parque Eduardo VII. Not far from here, further west, are upmarket **Rato** and **Amoreiras**.

Elegance: Jardim Botânico da Ajuda (p27)

Back at Praça do Comércio, a short distance east along the Rio Tejo is Santa Apolónia train station, where you'll also find some cool clubs and restaurants. Further east still, by the Ponte de Vasco da Gama, is Parque das Nações, site of Expo '98, with its spectacular Gare do Oriente and Oceanário.

To the west of Praça do Comércio are **Cais do Sodré**, **Doca de Alcântara** and **Doca de Santo Amaro**, under the Ponte 25 de Abril, with their waterfront restaurants and bars. Further west is beautiful **Belém**, the destination for museums and sights.

Itineraries

You can follow some very distinctive itineraries when visiting Lisbon. We've themed them here to help you make the most of your trip, but make sure you check out the Highlights chapter (p8) as well as Trips & Tours (p33), for day-trip suggestions.

HISTORY & ROMANCE

Take tram 28 via Sé Cathedral (p9) to Castelo de São Jorge (p8) for Lisbon vistas. Lunch outdoors at Casa do Leão (p52) then explore labyrinthine Alfama alleys. Have sunset drinks at Largo das Portas do Sol (p60), then a romantic dinner at Olivier (p52) and dancing at Lux (p65).

CULTURE & TRADITION

Observe tile-making traditions at Museu Nacional do Azulejo (p16) and artisans working at Museu de Artes Decorativas (p21). Lunch at wonderful Terreiro do Paço (p50) then soak up Lisbon's literary life at Café A Brasileira (p59); observe Portuguese puppeteering at Museu da Marioneta (p32) and sample port at Solar do Vinho do Porto (p63). Rest before dinner and *fado* (p60).

WORST OF LISBON

- Lisbon's hills offer wonderful views. Accessing them is like step-aerobics classes. Every day.
- Enough doggie-done-it on the streets to make a Parisian proud...
- Ho-hum restaurants on the beautiful pedestrianised streets of Baixa.
- *Bacalhau* – we love cod, but after a few days you start to miaow.

DAY OF DISCOVERY

See Belém's stunning Padrão dos Descobrimentos (p26), Torre de Belém (p26) and magical Mosteiro dos Jerónimos (p10), commemorating da Gama's voyage. Lunch at Belém or head to Parque das Nações (p19) to eat overlooking Ponte de Vasco da Gama (p26). Visit Oceanário (p19) before sinking a beer to high-seas adventure at Cervejaria da Trindade (p51).

Whimsical white watchtower: Torre de Belém (p26)

Highlights

CASTELO DE SÃO JORGE (4, A1)

The intriguing sight of St George's Castle, prettily perched on top of Lisbon's highest hill and splendidly lit at night, is what lures most visitors here. Its extraordinary history, told through the slick multimedia show, Olisipónia, is compelling. But it's really the spectacular views of the city and Rio Tejo (Tagus River) below that are most engaging.

The castle's first foundations were laid in 138 BC but it wasn't until the Moors arrived in 711, remaining settled for the next 400 years, that the citadel was fortified and a mosque was built. After the dramatic four-month Siege of Lisbon (1147) the fortress was sacked and recaptured by the Christian crusaders on their way to the Holy Land. The Castelo was transformed into a royal residence by King Afonso, but sadly went to ruin in the 17th century after a more sumptuous palace was built on Praça do Comércio.

Stroll through the leafy courtyards of olive and cork trees (once home to the Moorish elite, now inhabited by birds) and amble along the ramparts while admiring the views. Leave time to explore the atmospheric cobblestone streets of the charming Santa Cruz neighbourhood within the castle walls.

INFORMATION

- ☎ 218 800 620
- 🖳 www.egeac.pt in Portuguese
- ✉ Porta de São Jorge, Rua do Chão da Feira, Castelo
- € €3/1.50
- 🕙 castle & Olisipónia 9am-8.30pm, Camera Obscura 11am-2pm 15 Mar–15 Sep
- ℹ multilingual multimedia kiosks; book tours (departing every 30min) in advance
- 🚍 28
- ♿ fair
- ✗ Casa do Leão (p52)

DON'T MISS

- The camera obscura with its 360-degree live images of Lisbon
- The bust of Martim Moniz, who gave his life during the Siege of Lisbon
- Checking out Santa Cruz' fascinating courtyards

Castelo de São Jorge's towers keeping watch over Lisbon

SÉ CATHEDRAL (4, A2)

Victorious King Afonso built this sanctimonious Romanesque cathedral after the 1147 Siege of Lisbon, on the site of the Moor's main mosque.

Although this somewhat imposing structure is rock-solid in appearance, looks are deceiving – the Sé (meaning 'See' or 'Seat of a Bishop') experienced major damage during several tremors and was then destroyed in the 1755 earthquake, and there is little that remains of King Joao's wonderful 18th-century embellishments.

The proud cathedral is austere in overall appearance and the renovated nave becomes rather spooky when light and shadow have their way. But it's really the fine details and flourishes that are most memorable, such as the pretty stained-glass 'rose window' and the wonderful hand-carved 14th-century sarcophagi.

The crumbling 13th-century Gothic cloister houses extensive archaeological excavations, which include Roman stonework, a medieval cistern and some Moorish foundations.

The restored treasury contains some arresting illustrated manuscripts, pieces in silver, statues and robes. There are also relics here that Afonso brought to Lisbon in 1173 in a boat that, according to legend, was piloted by two ravens. They say the ravens' descendants protected the church, until the last one sadly died recently.

INFORMATION

- ☎ 218 866 752
- 🖳 www.ippar.pt
- ✉ Largo da Sé, Alfama
- € cathedral free, treasury €2.50, cloister €2.50
- ⌚ cathedral 9am-7pm Tue-Sat, to 5pm Mon & Sun; treasury 10am-5pm Mon-Sat; cloister 10am-5pm Mon May-Sep, to 6.30pm Tue-Sat, to 5pm Mon-Sat Oct-Apr
- 🚇 28
- ♿ limited (cathedral only)
- 🍴 Restô (p53)

The night-time glow of the Sé Cathedral

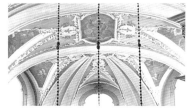

DON'T MISS

- The sarcophagi of a bearded nobleman, his wife and his dog
- The terrific tiled scene in the Franciscan chapel
- The 13th-century wrought-iron gate

MOSTEIRO DOS JERÓNIMOS (2, A3)

The flamboyance that typifies Manueline architecture reflected the extravagance of the time, especially that of Dom Manuel I himself, who commissioned the construction of this marvellous *mosteiro* (monastery) to celebrate Vasco da Gama's triumphant return following his discovery of the sea route to India. It was fitting that a 'pepper tax' on income from the spice trade helped finance the lavish project.

INFORMATION

- ☎ 213 620 034
- 🖥 www.mosteirojeronimos.pt
- ✉ Praça do Império, Belém
- € €3/1.50
- 🕐 10am-5pm Tue-Sun Oct-Apr, 10am-6pm Tue-Sun May-Sep
- 🚋 15
- 🚌 27, 28
- 🚆 Belém (Cascais line)
- ♿ limited
- 🍴 Caseiro (p56)

Cloisters of Mosteiro dos Jerónimos

Although building of the monastery began in 1501 (on the site of a riverside chapel where da Gama and his men prayed before sailing), it wasn't finished until 1541. The water has long since receded.

Early work followed Diogo de Boitaca's Gothic plans, but after his death in 1517 Spaniard João de Castilho gave the design a Renaissance flavour. Successive embellishments came with classical touches from Diogo de Torralva and Jerónimo de Ruão. In the 19th century a bell tower and enormous neo-Manueline wing were added to house the Order of St Jerome monks, whose mission was to pray for the souls of kings and sailors.

Dedicated to the Virgin Mary, who is also known as St Mary of Bethlehem (Belém), this wonderful *mosteiro*, with its spectacular vaulting, golden stone cloisters and intricately carved columns, is the finest example of the high-spirited Manueline style, and has become a Unesco World Heritage site.

DON'T MISS

- Exuberant detail of the South Portal
- Tombs of Manuel I, Vasco da Gama, poet Luís de Camões, writer Fernando Pessoa and historian Alexandre Herculano
- Splendid church views from the upper choir

BELÉM (2, A3)

Beautiful Belém is arguably the most pleasurable place to spend a day in Lisbon, with its great waterside location, absorbing museums, exuberant architecture, grand squares and exotic tropical gardens. Not to mention all those sunny outdoor restaurants and tasty *pastéis de Belém* (custard tarts) to reward your efforts!

Every intricately carved brick and *azulejo* (hand-painted tile) is imbued with the exciting spirit of Portugal's Age of Discovery. If only these Manueline walls could talk! After all it was from Belém's shores that many of the world's greatest adventurers – Magellan, Bartolomeu Dias, Pedro Alvares Cabral, Vasco da Gama – set sail and where their seafaring achievements were celebrated in style.

Most people come to see the elaborate Manueline architecture of the Mosteiro dos Jerónimos as well as its fascinating resident museums, **Museu de Marinha** (p22) and **Museu Nacional de Arqueologia** (p23). However, no two structures symbolise Portugal's maritime success more than the splendid

INFORMATION

- ✉ Avenida da Índia, Rua dos Jeronimos & Rua de Belém
- ☾ sights closed Mon
- 🚋 15
- 🚌 27, 28
- 🚉 Belém (Cascais line)
- ♿ good
- 🍴 snacks at Pastéis de Belém (p60), meals at Caseiro (p56)

DON'T MISS

- The incredible Visigothic jewellery collection at the Museu Nacional de Arqueologia (p23)
- Museu Nacional dos Coche's (p23) sumptuous royal carriages
- Centro Cultural de Belém's cool Museu do Design (p22)

Torre de Belém (p26) and its dramatic neighbour, the **Padrão dos Descobrimentos** (Monument to the Discoveries; p26), both of which are equally as enjoyable to visit.

When you're done exploring, rest your weary legs with the peacocks under **Jardim Botânico da Ajuda**'s shady palms.

Streetside cafés of Belém

ALFAMA (4)

Lively Alfama – with its jumble of steep, narrow cobbled lanes, jammed with skinny houses with lines of fluttering laundry strung between them – is more Arabic than European.

Alfama's 400 years of rich Moorish heritage is evident in more than just its medina-like streets – its name derives from the Arabic *al-hama*, meaning 'bath', and is inspired by the hot springs near Largo das Alcaçarias. This vibrant enclave skirting Castelo de São Jorge is Lisbon's oldest.

INFORMATION

- 28
- limited (very hilly, uneven paving)
- Malmequer Bemmequer (p53)

After the Christian reconquest of Lisbon, King Afonso rebuilt the castle into a royal residence, making Alfama a desirable address. Although its wealthy inhabitants moved away for fear of imminent earthquakes, Alfama's solid foundations, built into one big rock, meant that it stayed largely intact after the 1755 calamity. After the rich moved out, the working class moved in – mostly fishing-folk because of its proximity to the ports – giving this colourful neighbourhood the animated atmosphere it has today.

While there are interesting museums and charming churches to explore, it's just as pleasurable to wander the streets. Drop in to the friendly hole-in-the-wall grocery stores, haggle for bric-a-brac in the flea market, take lunch in traditional tavernas, and chill out with

DON'T MISS

- Museu de Artes Decorativas' fascinating collection (p21)
- Eclectic wares at Feira da Ladra (Thieves Market; p46)
- Miradouro de Santa Luzia's magical vistas

the kissing couples and old men playing cards on the *miradouros* (vantage points) with marvellous views of Lisbon and the Tejo.

Alfama viewed from Largo das Portas do Sol (p60)

MUSEU CALOUSTE GULBENKIAN (2, C2)

Almost as intriguing as this superb museum's outstanding collection of art is the man who bequeathed it to the Portuguese nation, along with a charitable foundation.

Born in Istanbul in 1869, Calouste Sarkis Gulbenkian was a very wealthy, and generous, Armenian oil magnate. Looking for neutral territiory during WWII, he moved to Portugal and made his home there. Living in Lisbon's Hotel Aviz for a decade, he became one of the 20th century's most generous and astute philanthropists. Gulbenkian's greatest coup was buying art from St Petersburg's Hermitage Museum in the late 1920s, when the new Soviet Union needed cash.

The finest museum in Lisbon (and one of the best in Europe) displays an exquisite and eclectic collection spanning every major epoch of Western and Eastern art. The building's sleek, purpose-built structure houses over 6000 pieces (of which only 1500 can be exhibited at any one time), and is wonderfully designed with light-filled rooms and surrounding tranquil gardens.

The rich collection of works includes Egyptian treasures, such as a 2700-year-old alabaster bowl, classical objects including Hellenic coins and Roman glassware; Oriental art, carpets, textiles and ceramics. The museum houses much European art from the 14th to 19th centuries, with impressive work by Rembrandt, Van Dyck, Rubens, Gainsborough, Turner, Rodin, Manet, Monet and Renoir, along with French furnishings, decorative art, glassware and incredible jewellery.

INFORMATION

- ☎ 217 823 000
- 🖥 www.museu.gulbenkian.pt
- ✉ Avenida de Berna 45a, São Sebastião
- € €3/free, Sun free, incl Centro de Arte Moderna €5
- ⏱ 10am-6pm Tue-Sun
- ℹ bilingual information touch-screens, booklet
- Ⓜ São Sebastião
- 🚌 46
- ♿ excellent
- ✖ café at museum

DON'T MISS

- A 2400-year-old Attic vase
- Armenian illuminated manuscripts
- enormous 18th-century Chinese porcelain
- René Lalique's fabulous Art Nouveau jewellery

CENTRO DE ARTE MODERNA (2, C2)

Gallery-goers will appreciate this consummate collection of modern and contemporary Portuguese art at the Calouste Gulbenkian Foundation's stunning Modern Art Centre, which adjoins Museu Calouste Gulbenkian (p13).

INFORMATION

- ☎ 217 823 474
- 🖳 www.camjap.gulbenkian.org
- ✉ Rua Dr Nicolau de Bettencourt, São Sebastião
- € €3/free, Sun free, incl Museu Calouste Gulbenkian €5
- 🕒 10am-6pm Tue-Sun
- ⓘ brochure
- Ⓜ São Sebastião
- 🚌 46
- ♿ good
- 🍴 café at museum

DON'T MISS

- Captivating colourful acrylics by Pedro Calapez
- Helena Almeida's beguiling black-and-white photographic work *Tela Habitada* (Inhabited Canvas)
- The sensuous Henry Moore sculpture in the garden

In 1983, when the museum first opened in its dazzling light-filled home, it was Lisbon's first exhibition space solely devoted to Portuguese art. Remaining the country's most important space for this purpose, it shows around 300 of 6000 works at any one time. The Centro de Arte Moderno's exhibits encompass drawing, painting, sculpture, photography, video and installation.

The permanent collection here includes many names synonymous with Portugal's modern-art movement. These include artists such as Amadeo de Souza Cardoso (a friend of Modigliani's whose work is characterised by experimentation in cubism, abstractionism, futurism and expressionism) and José de Almada Negreiros (the postcubist and abstract artist, who was formerly a dancer, graphic designer, illustrator and novelist, and who also experimented with tapestry, tiles and mosaic!).

The museum's Modern Art Centre prides itself on its collection featuring artists who had close ties with or were influences on Portuguese artists, such as Sonia and David Delaunay. Its other great claim is its collection of modern British art from the last 40 years of the 20th century, including work by David Hockney, Antony Gormley and Julian Opie. Another, unusual, highlight is a small but insightful Armenian collection – keep a look out for artist Arshile Gorky.

MUSEU NACIONAL DE ARTE ANTIGA (5, B6)

Lisbon has historically seen itself as Europe's gateway to the world and nowhere is this more apparent than in the National Museum of Ancient Art, a splendid collection spanning seven centuries of art, from 12th-century Portuguese developments to 19th-century romanticism.

Explorers, traders and missionaries set sail from Belém's shores and their journeys, encounters in new lands and arrivals home were all imagined and recreated in paintings, drawings and sculptures. The most coveted document of the Age of Discovery is Nuno Gonçalves' altarpiece, *Adoration of St Vincent*, featuring King Afonso V, Queen Isabel and Henry the Navigator and other key players of the period.

Many of the magnificent pieces of gold jewellery, rich tapestries and textiles, Japanese screens, African ivories, Chinese porcelain and Goan furniture are objects traders brought back from voyages; much of the religious art has come from monasteries, convents and churches.

INFORMATION
- ☎ 213 912 800
- 🖥 www.mnarteantiga-ipmuseus.pt
- ✉ Rua das Janelas Verdes 9, Lapa
- € €3/1.50
- ⏰ 10am-6pm Wed-Sun, 10am-2pm Tue
- ℹ brochure
- 🚋 15
- 🚌 28
- ♿ good
- ✘ café at museum

DON'T MISS
- Gold relics brought back by Vasco da Gama
- 16th-century Namban screens depicting the Portuguese arrival in Japan
- Hieronymus Bosch's hallucinatory *Temptation of St Anthony*

Wonderful work exhibited in the Casa das Janelas Verdes, the former 17th-century palace of the Marquês de Pombal, includes paintings by Portuguese talents Gregório Lopes, Frei Carlos, Josefa de Obidos and Domingos António de Sequeira, along with work by Raphael, Piero della Francesca and Albrecht Dürer.

Silver figurines now at home in the Museu Nacional de Arte Antiga

MUSEU NACIONAL DO AZULEJO (2, E2)

Lovers of ceramic tiles will be spellbound by the beautiful National Tile Museum and its unique collection of Portugal's national treasure – the *azulejo*.

The variety and beauty of the intricate tiles on display in the lovely former 15th-century convent of Igreja de Nossa Senhora da Madre de Deus is extraordinary and impressive.

The richly decorated antique tiles are organised in chronological order so the observer can trace the history of tile making and development of decorative designs. There is representation of tiles from around the globe and their border crossings are evident, from the intertwining and interweaving of patterns on Moorish tiles visible in the Spanish ceramics to the familiar blue-and-white historical scenes of Portuguese tiles apparent on their Flemish cousins.

Many of the tiles are ingeniously exhibited in their original state, decorating walls, staircases and windows. There are also wonderful temporary exhibitions of antique ceramics, pottery, porcelain and vases.

The convent itself is a delight, with all its glorious Manueline features, graceful cloisters, elegant tiled courtyards and waterside location. Just as impressive is the opulent interior and gold altarpiece of the chapel.

INFORMATION

- ☎ 218 147 747
- 💻 www.mnazulejo-ipmuseus.pt
- ✉ Rua Madre de Deus 4
- € €3/1.50
- 🕐 10am-6pm Wed-Sun, 2-6pm Tue
- ℹ brochure
- 🚌 42, 59
- ♿ good
- 🍴 Casanova (p53)

DON'T MISS

- The 1000-tile display depicting the history of Lisbon
- The enthralling panorama of Lisbon before the 1755 earthquake
- The painted chapel ceiling

Stories unfold on *azulejo* displays, Museu Nacional do Azulejo

PANTEÃO NACIONAL DE SANTA ENGRACIA (4, C1)

Appearing on a thousand postcards, the enormous dome of the National Pantheon and Church of Santa Engracia dominates the Lisbon skyline and offers staggering city and Tejo views.

Stunningly situated on a slope overlooking the river, this unique example of Portuguese baroque architecture was named the National Pantheon in 1916 and now contains tombs and memorials to Portuguese presidents and important historic and literary figures. These figures include such names as famous *fadista* (*fado* singer) Amália (p80); poets Luís Vaz de Camões and João de Deus; writer Almeida Garrett; the architect of the Age of Discovery, Henry the Navigator; and explorers Vasco da Gama and Pedro Álvares Cabral. The freedom fighter, General Humberto Delgado, is also entombed here; he was assassinated by the secret police in 1965.

King Manuel's daughter, Princess Mary, had commissioned construction of Igreja de Santa Engrácia in 1568, yet work on the stately edifice didn't begin until 1683 (long after Mary's death). The construction was still incomplete when its architect, João Antunes, died in 1712. Work continued, although the church was partially destroyed by the 1755 earthquake. Princess Mary's commission wasn't properly finished until the completion of its dome and inauguration in 1966. It took almost 400 years for this princess's wish to be granted!

INFORMATION
- ☎ 218 854 820
- 🖳 www.ippar.pt
- ✉ Campo de Santa Clara, Alfama
- € €2/1/0.80
- ⏱ 10am-5pm Tue-Sun
- ⓘ tours
- 🚋 28
- 🚌 9, 46
- ♿ good
- 🍴 Malmequer Bemmequer (p53)

DON'T MISS
- Light streaming through the dome onto the colourful mosaics
- Checking out the view of the interior on the way to the roof
- Splendid rooftop views of Alfama and Rio Tejo

BASÍLICA DA ESTRÉLA (5, B4)

Portugal's princesses had an unusual habit of commissioning the construction of churches. Princess Mary never got to see building of her Igreja de Santa Egrácia commence (see p17). Maria I, the daughter of King José I, promised to build a basilica if she gave birth to a son and heir. She had her son, and the building of her church began in 1779, but sadly the child died of smallpox before the basilica was completed in 1790.

INFORMATION

- ☎ 213 960 915
- ✉ Praça da Estréla, Estréla
- € free; nativity scene per 2min €0.50, per 4min €1
- ⏱ 8am-12.15pm & 3-8pm Mon-Sat, 9am-noon & 3-8pm Sun
- 🚌 28
- 🚋 9
- ♿ fair
- 🍴 Pão de Canela (p60)

Like the Igreja de Santa Egrácia, the Basílica da Estréla has a colossal dome, a wonderful marble interior and fantastic views over Lisbon and the river. With its combination of baroque and neoclassical influences, it is less stately and yet more elegant than Egrácia, with its pretty belfries, ornate decoration and statuary on the exterior. However, what makes Estréla really special is its richly detailed grey, pink and lemon patterned interior.

Outside, the peace and quiet of pretty Jardim da Estréla is sometimes punctuated by a lively brass band, while on Saturdays the garden often provides a lovely background for wedding pictures of Lisboan bridal parties.

DON'T MISS

- The spectacular dome view, rivalling Santa Egrácia's
- Asking to see Machado de Castro's bizarre cork-and-terracotta nativity scene
- Relaxing in tranquil Jardim da Estréla

Rich interior detail of Basílica da Estréla

PARQUE DAS NAÇÕES & OCEANÁRIO DE LISBOA (2, F3)

Situated northeast of the centre, on the Rio Tejo, Parque das Nações (Nations Park; pronounced naz-*oish*) was created as the site for the 1998 World Expo, successfully attracting over 10 million people (more than the population of Portugal!).

Established on reclaimed industrial wasteland that was formerly home to an oil refinery, abattoir and rubbish dump, the project transformed the face of the waterfront from eyesore to spectacular architectural playground.

With the 150 Expo pavilions long gone, what's left behind is a landscaped riverside park with some terrific sights, such as leading architect Álvaro Siza Vieira's **Pavilhão de Portugal**. There's also the 140m-high Vasco da Gama Tower (currently closed), the incredibly strong **Ponte de Vasco da Gama** (p26), some waterside eateries and bars, an excellent shopping mall and stunning apartment and office blocks.

The favourite for many people is Oceanário de Lisboa, the seven-million-litre aquarium, with a vast central tank containing five million litres of water. It's home to 450 species of sea life from the world's seas, including creatures such as a 2.5m-wide giant manta, adorable otters, affable penguins, and not-so-friendly sharks. Children also love the nearby **Pavilhão do Conhecimento** (Pavilion of Knowledge; p32).

INFORMATION

- ☎ 218 919 333
- 🖥 www.parquedasnacoes.pt, www.oceanario.pt
- ✉ Ave Dom Joao II, Parque das Nações
- € Cartão do Parque incl Oceanário, Pavilhão do Conhecimento, Teleférico & discounts on bikes, bowling & dining €15.50/8.50, Oceanário €9/4.50, Teleférico €5.50/3
- ⏲ Oceanário 10am-7pm Apr-Oct, 10am-6pm Nov-Mar; Teleférico 11am-7pm
- ℹ Posto de Informação 10am-8pm Apr-Oct, 10am-7pm Nov-Mar, free maps and information
- Ⓜ Oriente
- ♿ good
- 🍴 Agua e Sal (p57)

DON'T MISS

- Admiring the Santiago Calatreva–designed Gare do Oriente
- Interacting at Pavilhão do Conhecimento
- Awesome views from the Teleférico (cable car)

SÃO VICENTE DE FORA (4, B1)

Founded in 1147, this beautiful church and monastery (called St Vincent of Outside, as it was outside the city walls) was built on the burial sites of foreign crusaders and later, between 1582 and 1629, reconstructed under the guidance of Italian Renaissance master, Felipe Terzi. While the main dome and roof collapsed on worshippers in the earthquake of 1755, it was later rebuilt. The style of the façade was the first of its kind in the country and it informed many 17th-century façades throughout the Portuguese sphere of influence.

INFORMATION

- ☎ 218 824 400
- 🖳 www.ippar.pt
- ✉ Calçada de São Vicente, Alfama
- € €4/2
- ⏱ 9am-6pm Mon-Sat, 9am-12.30pm & 3-5pm Sun & Aug
- ⓘ brochure
- 🚃 28
- ♿ fair
- 🍴 Malmequer Bemmequer (p53)

The adjoining monastery is famous for its remarkable blue-and-white *azulejos* (14,521 of them) dating from the 18th century. Up on the 1st floor, there's a unique collection of 38 panels depicting La Fontaine's fables (entertaining 17th-century moral tales), with accompanying English and French background text. At the rear of the monastery is the former refectory that was transformed into the Bragança Mausoleum in 1885. This sombre room contains the marble tombs of most of the Braganças (former rulers of Portugal). But perhaps the best part of the visit is the expansive views of the Rio Tejo after you climb the stairs to the roof.

DON'T MISS

- The lone, stone mourning woman at the tomb of Carlos I and his son Luís Felipe
- The view of Ponte de Vasco da Gama from the far edge of the roof
- The altar and carved wooden statues in the church

Overhead of Mosteiro de São Vicente de Fora

Sights & Activities

MUSEUMS & GALLERIES

Casa do Fado e da Guitarra Portuguesa
(4, B2)
Melancholy *fado* is so intrinsic to Portuguese culture that visiting this vibrant museum is a must, to learn about the music, its working-class Alfama roots and to pick up some CDs. We love the kitsch dioramas and recreation of a *fado* house, although it feels odd that you can't order a drink!
☎ 218 823 470 ⬚ www.egeac.pt/casadofado in Portuguese ✉ Largo do Chafariz de Dentro, Alfama € €2.50/1.25 ⏱ 10am-6pm 🚌 28, 59

Casa Museu de Amália Rodrigues
(5, C4)
The greatest *fadista*, Amália (see p80), lived in this wonderful house, which has become a place of pilgrimage for the Portuguese. On the short multilingual tour you'll get to see her costumes, jewellery and awards, and listen to her soulful music.
☎ 213 971 896 ✉ Rua de São Bento 193, São Bento € €5 ⏱ 10am-1pm & 2-6pm Tue-Sun Ⓜ Rato

Centro Cultural de Belém
(2, A3)
The exhibition centre at Lisbon's most dynamic cultural venue hosts adventurous contemporary art, sculpture, photography, architecture and mixed-media exhibitions and installations, and a very cool Museu do Design (p22), along with innovative programmes of modern dance, music and theatre,

Portuguese guitars, Museu de Musica (p22)

and some wonderful galleries and shops.
☎ 213 612 400 ⬚ www.ccb.pt ✉ Praça do Império, Belém € €5/2.50, incl design museum €7.50 ⏱ 10am-7pm Tue-Sun 🚊 15 🚌 27, 28 🚉 Belém (Cascais line)

Museu Arqueológico do Carmo
(6, B3)
This small museum in the sacristy of the Convento do Carmo ruins was established to protect the convent's ancient religious relics, following Portugal's abolition of all religious orders in 1834. It has an exceptional, albeit small, collection of ancient coins, prehistoric implements, carved tombs, and mummies!
☎ 213 460 473 ✉ Largo do Carmo, Baixa € €2.50/free ⏱ 10am-6pm Mon-Sat Apr-Sep, 10am-5pm Oct-Mar

Museu da Carris
(3, A2)
Through an engaging display of historic trams, buses, photographs, uniforms and tickets, this fascinating museum successfully brings to life the history of transportation in the city, beginning with Lisbon's adoption of Rio de Janeiro's tram system. Don't miss the vintage tram ride to check out the historic trams.
☎ 213 613 087 ⬚ www.carris.pt in Portuguese ✉ Rua Primeiro de Maio, Lapa € €2.50/1.25 ⏱ 10am-1pm & 2-5pm Mon-Sat 🚊 15 🚌 27, 42, 56

Museu da Cidade
The compelling City Museum, in the Palácio Pimenta, vividly tells the story of Lisbon's evolution through photographs, documents, wonderful tiles, and an enormous model of pre-earthquake Lisbon. Look out for the peacocks wandering around the courtyard.
☎ 217 513 200 ✉ Campo Grande 245, Campo Grande € €2 ⏱ 10am-1pm & 2-6pm Tue-Sun Ⓜ Campo Grande

Museu de Artes Decorativas
(4, B2)
This brilliant museum and school of decorative arts, operated by the Fundação Ricardo do Espírito Santo Silva, displays 15th- to 19th-century

SIGHT TIMES

When planning your itinerary, keep in mind that Lisbon's museums and sights are generally closed on Mondays and all public holidays. Also worth noting is that many of these shut for lunch, making planning your day more akin to planning a military exercise. Also, many smaller museums may not stick to the advertised schedule; in other words they may open late or not at all on the days advertised. On the bright side, many of the sights listed are often free on the last Sunday of every month.

furniture, textiles, jewellery, silverware and porcelain in an aristocratic 18th-century palace. Call ahead to see the workshops where artisans practise traditional wood carving, cabinet making, metal work, book binding, decorative painting, gilding, rug making, glassware, furniture and porcelain restoration and more. ☎ 218 862 183 ☐ www .fress.pt ✉ Largo das Portas do Sol 2, Alfama ⊙ 10am-5pm ☒ 15 ☒ 27, 28 ☒ Belém (Cascais line)

Museu de Marinha
(2, A3)
Even non-nautical people will find this maritime naval museum intriguing, with its armadas of full-size and model ships, ornate royal barges, navigational equipment, fabulous statues, wonderful maps, paintings, old black-and-white photographs and exquisite relics brought back from voyages. ☎ 213 620 019 ☐ http://museu.marinha.pt in Portuguese ✉ Mosteiro dos Jerónimos, Praça do Império Belém € €3/1.50 ⊙ 10am-5pm Tue-Sun Oct-Mar, 10am-6pm Apr-Sep ☒ 15 ☒ 27, 28 ☒ Belém (Cascais line)

Museu de Musica (2, B1)
Music buffs will love this small museum's splendid collection – one of the best in Europe – of more than a thousand truly exquisite musical instruments from the 16th to the 20th century. Highlights include extremely rare and unique pieces, such as a piano that belonged to Franz Liszt and an outstanding collection of stringed instruments. ☎ 217 710 999 ☐ www .museudamusica-ipmuseus .pt ✉ Metro Alto dos Moinhos, Rua Joao de Frietas Branco, Benfica € €2 ⊙ 10am-6pm Tue-Sat ⓜ Alto dos Moinhos

Museu do Chiado (6, B4)
Lisbon's Museu Nacional de Arte Contemporânea (MNAC), situated in the stunningly renovated Convento de São Francisco, has a superb permanent collection of modern Portuguese art, spanning romanticism, surrealism, abstract art and new realism, plus some superb temporary exhibitions of contemporary art and photography. ☎ 213 432 148 ☐ www .museudochiado-ipmuseus .pt ✉ Rua Serpa Pinto 4, Chiado € €3/1.50 ⊙ 10am-6pm Tue-Sun ⓜ Baixa-Chiado ☒ 28

Museu do Design (2, A3)
This superlative design museum, in the Centro Cultural de Belém (p21), displays furniture and product design from the 1930s to the present. This very cool collection features the masters – Capelo, Panton, Gehry, Starck, Newson and the Eames – and there are

Eames chairs in the Museu do Design

frequent temporary shows and a decent bookshop.

☎ 213 612 400 ⬜ www .ccb.pt in Portuguese ✉ Praça do Império, Belém € €3.50/1.25, incl Centro Cultural de Belém Exhibitions €7.50 ⏲ 10am-7pm Tue-Sun 🚊 15 🚌 27, 28 🚃 Belém (Cascais line)

Museu do Palácio Nacional da Ajuda (2, B3)

The grand neoclassical Museum of the Royal Palace building replaced the original, destroyed by fire in 1795, used until the royal family went into exile in Brazil in 1807. It was not used again until King Luis I married an Italian princess in 1861 and lavished it with the riches that can be seen today. The Winter Garden is wonderful!

☎ 213 637 095 ⬜ www .ippar.pt/monumentos /palacio_ajuda.html in Portuguese ✉ Largo da Ajuda, Ajuda € €4/2 ⏲ 10am-5pm Thu-Tue, 1-hr guided tours every 30min 🚌 27, 42

Museu do Teatro Romano (4, A2)

This museum was created in 2002 to display the city's ruined Roman theatre. Built during Emperor Augustus' time, the theatre was extended in AD 57 to seat up to 5000, until it was abandoned in the 4th century so its stones could be used to build the city. As little is left to look at, the museum very cleverly inspires the visitor to reimagine the monument.

☎ 217 513 200 ✉ Pátio do Aljube 5, Baixa ⏲ 10am-1pm & 2-6pm Tue-Sun 🚊 28

Cinderella's ride: gilded coach, Museu Nacional dos Coches

Museu Militar (4, C2)

One for history/military buffs, the former Royal Army Arsenal is now the National Military Museum, hosting one of the largest collections of artillery in the world — cannons, pistols, guns and swords, along with related paintings, sculpture, drawings and tiles.

☎ 218 842 300; ✉ Largo do Museu de Artilharia, Santa Apolónia € €2.50/1 ⏲ 10am-6pm Tue-Sun 🚊 28 🚌 9

Museu Nacional de Arqueologia (2, A3)

The impressive National Museum of Archaeology, in the Mosteiro dos Jerónimos, has some beautifully lit collections of Bronze Age objects, ornaments and jewellery, along with Egyptian antiquities and an exciting programme of temporary exhibitions.

☎ 213 620 000 ⬜ www .mnarqueologia-ipmuseus.pt ✉ Mosteiro dos Jerónimos, Praça do Império, Belém € €3/1.50 ⏲ 10am-6pm Wed-Sun 2-6pm Tue 🚊 15 🚌 27, 28 🚃 Belém (Cascais line)

Museu Nacional dos Coches (2, A3)

All that glitters *is* gold here. In the former royal riding school, the sumptuous National Coach Museum has a spectacular collection of gilded 17th- to 19th-century carriages and coaches that belonged to Portugal's royals — they're jaw-dropping. Our fave is the 18th-century Cinderella-like Coach of the Oceans.

☎ 213 610 850 ⬜ www .museudoscoches-ipmuseus .pt ✉ Praça Afonso de Albuquerque, Belém € €3/1.50 ⏲ 10am-5.30pm Tue-Sun 🚊 15 🚌 27, 28 🚃 Belém (Cascais line)

Palácio Nacional da Ajuda

Museu Nacional do Teatro

You won't need to know anything about Portuguese drama to find the National Theatre Museum fascinating. It houses a beguiling collection of 300,000 pieces, with wonderful theatrical costumes, props, set dressing, models of sets, drawings, posters, programmes, postcards, scripts, photos and music scores. It's near the Museu Nacional do Traje e da Moda (below), and is set in the lush Parque de Monteiro Mór.

☎ 217 567 410 ⌨ www .museudoteatro-ipmuseus .pt ✉ Estrada d Lumiar 10-12, Parque de Monteiro Mór, Lumiar € incl Museu Nacional do Traje e da moda €3/1.50 ☯ 10am-6pm Tue-Sun Ⓜ Lumiar 🚌 36

Museu Nacional do Traje e da Moda

The National Costume and Fashion Museum has a fabulous collection of some 7000 costumes and accessories from the Middle Ages to the present, and a fantastic exhibition on the textile-making process, with real looms in action and weaving and tapestry workshops. There's a sensual exhibition for the blind based on touching, smelling and listening to the textiles!

☎ 217 590 318 ⌨ www .museudotraje-ipmuseus.pt ✉ Largo Júlio de Castilho, Parque de Monteiro Mór, Lumiar € incl Museu Nacional do Teatro €3/1.50 ☯ 10am-6pm Tue-Sun Ⓜ Lumiar 🚌 36

Palácio Fronteira (2, B1)

This beautiful 17th-century palace influenced by the Italian Renaissance was initially built as a hunting lodge, around 1670, on what was once the outskirts of the city. The fifth Marquês de Fronteira moved here full-time after the downtown dwelling was destroyed by the 1755 earthquake. The fascinating tour of the palace takes you through the wonderful terracotta pink building, which features some brilliant *azulejos* (tiles), especially in the 'battle room', with its battle depictions. There is a lovely terrace and magnificent formal gardens where you can wander around after the tour. Arrive at least 15 minutes before the tour start time.

☎ 217 782 023 ✉ Largo São Domingos de Benfica 1, Sete Rios € €5.50 ☯ by guided tour only, at 10.30am, 11am, 11.30am & noon Mon-Sat Jun-Sep, 11am & noon Oct-May Ⓜ Jardim Zoológico, then taxi

NOTABLE BUILDINGS & MONUMENTS

Aqueduto das Águas Livres (2, B1)

The 18km-long grey stone aqueduct, constructed between 1728 and 1835 on the order of Dom João V, brought the city its first clean drinking water. Having withstood the 1755 earthquake, its 109 arches cross Lisbon's hills, most dramatically at Campolide, where it is 65m high. It's possible to take a tour of the aqueduct, through the Museu da Água (p31).

☎ 218 135 522 ✉ Campolide 🚌 from Rossio to Campolide

Campo Pequeno (2, D1)

Lisbon's red-brick Moorish-inspired bullfighting ring,

The 18km-long Aqueduto das Águas Livres

Francisco Franco's Cristo Rei

with its pretty cupola-topped towers, was built in 1892, but is currently closed for renovation. When it was open, it could hold up to 9,000 people to see its weekly bullfights during the season. When it reopens, it will have an underground shopping mall and cinemas. ☎ 217 932 093 ⊠ Praça de Touros do Campo Pequeno, Avenida da República, Campo Pequeno Ⓜ Campo Pequeno

Casa dos Bicos (4, A3)
This whimsical 16th-century mansion was one of the few to survive the 1755 earthquake. Built by Afonso de Albuquerque, former viceroy to India, it's known as the House of 'Points' or 'Spikes' because of its diamond-

Elevador de Santa Justa

shaped stone façade. As it's the offices for the Comemorações dos Descobrimentos organisation, the interior is not open to the public, unless the organisation is hosting a special event or exhibition. ⊠ Rua dos Bacalhoeiros 10, Alfama 🚊 28 🚌 9, 28, 46, 59

Cristo Rei
Lisbon's 28m-tall statue of Christ the King is clearly modelled on His more famous Rio de Janeiro cousin, Christ the Redeemer. Commissioned by Salazar, it was designed by Francisco Franco in 1949 and took 10 years to construct. If you're intrigued enough to venture to the south side of the Rio Tejo (Tagus River), you'll be rewarded with a lovely ferry ride and heavenly views from the statue's pedestal. ☎ 212 751 000 ⊠ Santuario Nacional do Cristo Rei, Alto do Pragal, Almada ☼ 9am-6pm ⚓ from Praça do Comércio or Cais do Sodré to Cacilhas, then bus 101

Elevador de Santa Justa (6, C3)
Connecting Baixa and Bairro Alto, this eccentric 45m-high cast-iron lift was designed by

Raul Mésnier du Ponsard, an apprentice to Gustave Eiffel. Steam-powered when it was completed in 1902, it was Lisbon's only public elevator. Don't miss the spectacular views of Lisbon and the Rio Tejo from the viewing platform and café. Apart from the view though, it's a pointless ride as you still can't cross the viaduct to Rua do Carmo due to long-term restoration work. ☎ 213 613 054 ⊠ Rua de Santa Justa & Rua Aurea, Baixa € €1.10 ☼ 9am-9pm Ⓜ Baixa-Chiado 🚊 28

Gare do Oriente (2, F2)
Fabulous Gare do Oriente was designed by world-renowned Spanish architect Santiago Calatrava. With the redevelopment of the area for the '98 Expo, this train station was to be many people's first glimpse of the Expo site and Calatrava. An engineer who gives priority to function over form, and famed for his open buildings and bridges, Calatrava created an airy vaulted structure with an almost skeletal frame. The metro station below features *azulejo* works by international artists. ⊠ Parque das Nações Ⓜ Oriente

ELEVATE ME

Besides the obligatory trip on tram 28, which winds its way from Anjos to Estrela like a Disney amusement ride, you should take the opportunity to ride the city's *ascensors* (funiculars). Of course, the most famous ride is the **Elevador de Santa Justa** (p25), but due to restoration works it's just an elevator with a pretty view – these other *ascensors* get you somewhere and save your suffering legs! The best ride is **Ascensor da Bica** (5, E5; ☺ 7am-9pm Mon-Sat, 9am-9pm Sun), which takes you through the Santa Catarina district at the southwest corner of the Bairro Alto. **Ascensor da Gloria** (6, B2; ☺ 7am-midnight Mon-Thu, 7am-12.30am Fri-Sat, 8am-midnight Sun) handily goes from Praça dos Restauradores up to the São Pedro de Alcântara viewpoint (check out how the *ascensor* stays level during the ride!). **Ascensor do Lavra** (5, E4; ☺ 7am-9pm Mon-Sat, 9am-9pm Sun) is the least used of the *ascensors*, but was the first of its type in the world (opening in 1884) and runs from Largo da Anunciada to Rua Câmara Pestana.

Padrão dos Descobrimentos (2, A3)

Inaugurated in 1960 on the 500th anniversary of Prince Henry the Navigator's death, the wonderful, enormous limestone Discoveries Monument is shaped like a caravel. Henry himself looks over the ship's prow, with explorers Vasco da Gama, Diogo Cão and Fernão de Magalhães behind him, along with a host of other Portuguese heroes, including poet Luís Vaz de Camões and painter Nuno Gonçalves. Inside you can watch the engaging audiovisual

Padrão dos Descobrimentos

programme, The Lisbon Experience.
☎ 213 031 957 ✉ Avenida de Brasília, Belém
€ €3/1.50 ☺ 10am-6pm Tue-Sun Oct-May, 10am-7pm Jun-Sep ⛴ 15 🚋 27, 28
🚆 Belém (Cascais line)

Palácio da Assembleia da República (5, C4)

Portugal's parliament, known as the Palácio da Assembleia Nacional, has convened since 1833 in the massive yet splendid Palácio de São Bento, once the 17th-century Benedictine convent of São Bento. Tours by appointment; book one day ahead.
☎ 213 919 000 ✉ Largo de Cortes, São Bento ⛴ 28
🚋 27

Ponte de Vasco da Gama

Another extraordinary Expo '98 initiative, this 17,185m-long and 30m-wide bridge is Europe's longest bridge, with foundations extending 85m below sea level. It has also been built to withstand 250kmph winds and an earthquake 4.5 times stronger than the 1755 calamity. A great vantage point from

where you can check it out is the Teleférico at the park.
✉ Parque das Nações
Ⓜ Oriente

Ponte 25 de Abril (3, A3)

Built in 1966 and originally named Ponte Salazar after the dictator who commissioned it, this suspension bridge, with its echoes of the Golden Gate Bridge in San Francisco, was renamed after the date of the revolution in 1974. At 2km, it was once one of the longest suspension bridges in Europe; its traffic jams were legendary before the building of the Ponte de Vasco da Gama, now they're merely awful. There are great views of the scale of the bridge from the Museu da Carris (p21).
✉ views from Lapa & Alcântara

Torre de Belém (2, A3)

One of Belém's highlights and another Unesco World Heritage Site, this whimsical white Manueline masterpiece was built in 1515 as an offshore watchtower to protect the city's harbour. Designed by Diogo and

Francisco Arruda for King Manuel I, it is wonderfully detailed with the flamboyant flourishes and maritime motifs of the Manueline style. Amazingly, it once sat midstream before the water line moved. Now you reach land by an unsightly modern footbridge.

☎ 213 620 034 ✉ Praça do Império, Avenida de Brasília, Belém € €3/2.70 ☼ 10am-5pm Tue-Sun 🚊 15 🚌 27, 28 🚃 Belém (Cascais line)

PARKS & PUBLIC SPACES

Avenida da Liberdade
(5, E3)
This grand avenue stretching from Praça dos Restauradores (p29) up to Praça Marquês de Pombal (p29) was completed, as it stands today, in 1882. Given the nonstop traffic that zooms past on either side of the tree-lined avenue, it's best imagined as it was back in the days when you could hear the tinkle of the fountains and enjoy its cafés without car fumes.

✉ Liberdade Ⓜ Restauradores, Avenida 🚌 9, 36, 45, 46, 91

Jardim Botânico (5, D3)
A wonderfully cool spot in summer, Lisbon University's botanic gardens has many exotic and wonderful old trees that shade your walk through it. Located within the gardens is the Museu de História Natural, which holds temporary exhibits and houses the Museu de Ciência (p32).

☎ 213 921 800 🖥 www .jb.ul.pt in Portuguese ✉ Rua da Escola Politécnica 58, Liberdade ☼ 9am-6pm Mon-Fri, 10am-6pm Sat & Sun Oct-Apr, to 8pm May-Sep € €1.50/0.60 Ⓜ Rato, Avenida 🚌 58

Jardim Botânico da Ajuda (2, A3)
These stately botanical gardens were the first of their kind in Lisbon. Domenico Vandelli, an Italian botanist who became the director of the gardens, laid them out in 1768. Under the instruction of

Parque Eduardo VII

King José I, Vandelli procured plants from all corners of the globe. Today, the flora is labelled and planted around orderly box-hedges.

☎ 213 622 503 ✉ Calçada da Ajuda, Ajuda ☼ Thu-Tue 9am-5pm, to 8pm May-Sep € €1.50/0.60 🚊 15 🚌 27, 28 🚃 Belém (Cascais line)

Jardim da Estrela (5, C4)
Opposite the Basílica da Estréla (p18), this delightful park fulfils the great-park check list: duck pond, café, lovely gardens, children's playground and a good old-fashioned bandstand.

✉ Praça da Estrela, Estrela ☼ 7am-midnight 🚊 28 🚌 9, 27

Parque Eduardo VII
(5, D1)
This massive sloping park was named in honour of England's Edward VII after a visit in 1903. While the gardens are somewhat under-utilised, the views from the top of the park are outstanding. There are two fascinating greenhouses filled with exotic flowers here as well: an *estufa fria* (cool

Domenico Vandelli's lush Jardim Botânico da Ajuda

MARQUÊS OF A MAN

Sebastião José de Carvalho e Melo, generally known as the Marquês de Pombal (1699–1782), is best known for his reconstruction efforts after the devastating 1755 earthquake and subsequent tsunami. When asked what to do after the destruction, the Marquês reputedly replied, 'We bury the dead and feed the living.' His no-nonsense approach as King José I's trusted prime minister saw central Lisbon being rebuilt within the year. A progressive but single-minded and ruthless leader, he subsequently muted the Portuguese Inquisition, ended slavery in Portugal and its colonies, and reorganised both the military and education systems. After being made Marquês de Pombal in 1770, his political authority and economic reforms did not sit well with Portugal's aristocracy, which already thought him too powerful. On King José I's death in 1779, Queen Maria I (his daughter), who disliked the Marquês, stripped him of his political power. His tomb is at the Igreja de Memória (p30).

greenhouse) and an *estufa quente* (hot greenhouse). ✉ Avenida da Liberdade, Marquês de Pombal ☀ cool greenhouse 9am-5pm Oct-Apr, to 6pm May-Sep; hot greenhouse 9am-4.30pm Oct-Apr, to 5.30pm May-Sep; gardens 9am-4.30pm Oct-Apr, to 5.30pm May-Sep Ⓜ Marquês de Pombal 🚌 12, 36

Praça da Figueira & Praça dom Pedro IV (Rossio) (6, C3)
These squares are lively focal points for visitors and locals alike. The larger Praça dom

King João I: Praça da Figueira

Pedro IV, also known as Rossio, was once the scene of animal markets, fairs, bullfights and worse during the Inquisition. The central statue is of Dom Pedro IV and on the northern side of the square is the restored 1846 Teatro Nacional de Dona Maria II. Praça da Figueira features a statue of King João I and innumerable pigeons, and was a marketplace until the 1950s.
✉ Baixa Ⓜ Rossio 🚌 9, 36, 45, 46, 91

Praça do Comércio (6, C5)
This grand square is still known by locals as Terreiro do Paço (Palace Square), after the royal palace that stood here until the 1755 earthquake. This wasn't the only tragedy to occur on this site. In 1908 the square witnessed the death knell of the monarchy, when King Carlos I and his son were assassinated by anarchists. The bronze equestrian statue is of King José I, the ruler at the time of the earthquake.
✉ Baixa Ⓜ Baixa-Chiado 🚋 15, 18 🚌 9, 36, 45, 46, 59, 91

Praça do Município (6, B5)
Somewhat overshadowed by the neighbouring Praça do Comércio, Praça do Municipio is an elegant square, dominated on the eastern side by the 1874 Paços do Concelho (Town Hall), designed by Domingos Parente. The republic was proclaimed from this square on 5 October 1910.
✉ Rua do Arsenal, Baixa Ⓜ Baixa-Chiado 🚋 15, 18 🚌 9, 36, 45, 46, 59, 91

Praça do Príncipe Real (5, D4)
This atmospheric, shady park is a wonderful retreat on a hot summer's day. In the late afternoon old men gather to play cards and dominoes, kids romp in the playground and lovers whisper in the picturesque café. Surprisingly located in the middle of the park is the Reservatório da Patriarcal, an underground water reservoir that was constructed between 1860 and 1864 and is part of the Museu da Água (p31).
🚋 Ascensor da Gloria

Praça dos Restauradores
(6, B2)
Easily identified by its distinctive obelisk (erected in 1886), the square honours the reestablishment of Portugal's independence from the Spanish in 1640 (*restauradores* means 'restoration'). The grand Palácio Foz (now headquarters for ICEP Turismo, see p89) is on the west side of the square, and a couple of doors down is the imposing Art Deco Teatro Eden (1937), now an apartment hotel, the VIP Eden (p72).
Ⓜ Restauradores ➌ 9, 36, 45, 46, 59, 91

Praça Marquês de Pombal
(5, D2)
On what is probably the busiest roundabout in Lisbon stands a massive monument to the Marquês de Pombal (p28), who ruled Portugal by proxy from 1750 to 1777. Standing atop the structure is a bronze of the man himself, with a lion for company, eyeing the Baixa in the distance and probably cursing the town planning that allowed the roundabout to be such a traffic magnet.
✉ Marquês de Pombal
Ⓜ Marquês de Pombal

Rua Augusta
(6, C4)
Perhaps no other street in Lisbon better captures the character of the charming Baixa. The view along this pedestrianised and mosaic-tiled street, towards the equestrian statue of King José I in Praça de Comércio, framed perfectly by the triumphal Arco de Victoria, is one of Lisbon's most enigmatic sights. The

Busy Praça Marquês de Pombal

downtown area is the centre of commerce, where shops, stalls and street performers compete for your attention.
✉ Baixa Ⓜ Baixa-Chiado
🚋 15, 18 ➌ 9, 36, 45, 46, 59, 91

CHURCHES & CATHEDRALS

Convento do Carmo
(6, B3)
With skeletal arches visible from many points of Lisbon, the ruins of this Carmelite convent stand as dramatic testimony to the 1755 earthquake. Once one of

Lisbon's largest churches, its only remains are the Gothic arches, walls and flying buttresses. It was built in 1423 under the orders of Nuno Álvares Pereira, Dom João I's military commander who became a member of the Carmelite order. The small Museu Arqueológico do Carmo (p21) is located here.
✉ Largo do Carmo, Chiado
Ⓜ Baixa-Chiado 🚋 28

Igreja de Graça
(2, D2)
While the monastery (dating from 1271 and rebuilt after the earthquake) is used as a military recruitment centre, this church is still in use and

Skeletal ruins: Convento do Carmo

Ornate interior of a side chapel, Igreja de São Roque

can be visited. Inside, the most important features are the 17th-century *azulejos* on the altar, while outside the attraction is the little café under the trees at the *miradouro* (vantage point), with its lovely views.
✉ Miradouro da Graça, Graça 🚋 28

Igreja de Memória
(2, A3)
A steep 10-minute walk or quick bus ride (bus 27) from Largo dos Jerónimos, this small neoclassical church was founded by King Jose I, after an unsuccessful attempt on his life. Retribution by the Marquês de Pombal (see p28) was exhaustive and members of the Távora family (whom the king had just visited) were executed – accused of a conspiracy. But it was also a convenient way for the Marquês de Pombal to shed some enemies. His tomb is the most notable feature of the church.
✉ Calcada do Galvao, Ajuda 🚋 15 🚌 27, 28 🚆 Belém (Cascais line)

Igreja de Santo António
(4, A2)
Across the road from the Sé Cathedral is the Church of St Anthony, said to be built on the site of the saint's birthplace. A crypt (on the left) purports to be this site and is one of the only features left after the earthquake destroyed the existing church. The small museum next door features countless statues, books and engravings from the 18th to 20th centuries, all devoted to Anthony, Lisbon's most popular saint.
☎ 218 869 145 ✉ Largo Santo Antonio a Sé, Alfama 🕒 10am-1pm & 2-6pm Tue-Sun € museum €1.20/0.60 🚋 28 🚌 37

Igreja de São Domingos
(6, C2)
This extraordinary church appears to really be blessed, surviving earthquakes in 1531 and 1755, and fire in 1959. It wears its battle scars in a multitude of ways and the interior is an absorbing sight, with fire-scorched, damaged stone pillars and the faint, still permeating smell.
✉ Largo de São Domingos, Baixa 🕒 7.30am-7pm M Rossio

Igreja de São Roque
(6, A3)
The unremarkable façade of this 16th-century Jesuit church masks the embarrassment of riches inside. The church consists of several chapels, the most notable (and extravagant) being the Capela de São João Baptista (Chapel of St John the Baptist). Commissioned in 1740 by King João V, it was built in Rome between 1742 and 1750, blessed by the pope, dismantled and shipped to Lisbon. The accompanying museum features religious artefacts.
☎ 213 235 383 ✉ Largo Trindade Coelho, Bairro Alto 🕒 church 8.30am-5pm, museum 10am-5pm Tue-Sun 🚋 Elevador da Glória 🚌 58

Nossa Senhora da Conceição Velha (4, A3)
The *portal* (door) of this church, which is located on the site of an old synagogue,

is all that remains of the Igreja de Nossa Senhora da Misericórdia, which was destroyed in the 1755 earthquake. The finely carved Manueline façade with its angels and flowers was rebuilt and later reattached to the church after the earthquake. You'd better watch out trying to get a good view of it – try not to get hit by a taxi on this busy street.

☎ 218 870 202 ✉ Rua da Alfândega, Baixa ✷ 8am-6pm Mon-Fri, 8am-4pm Sat, 10am-2pm Sun 🚊 18 🚌 9, 46

QUIRKY LISBON

Cemitério dos Ingleses (5, B4)

Across the road from the top entrance of the Jardim da Estréla (p27) is the British Cemetery, founded in 1717. It is notable as the burial place of novelist Henry Fielding, best known for his work *Tom Jones*. Fielding, who left London to better his health in 1753, died in Lisbon in 1754. At the far corner is all that remains of

Inner workings at Museu da Água

Lisbon's old Jewish cemetery. To enter the cemetery, you need to ring the buzzer to be let in.

☎ 213 906 248 ✉ Rua de São Jorge à, Estrela ✷ 9am-1pm Tue-Sun 🚊 28 🚌 9, 27

Museu da Água (2, D2)

Run by the municipal water company, Empresa Portuguesa das Águas Livres (EPAL), this award-winning museum is housed in the city's first steam-pumping station. Dedicated to the history of the supplying of

water to Lisbon from Roman times to the present day, it's far more engaging than you would expect. The museum also handles tours for the monumental Aqueduto das Águas Livres (p24).

☎ 218 100 215 🖳 www
.museudaagua.epal.pt ✉ Rua do Alviela 12, Santa Apolónia € €2.50/1.50 ✷ 10am-6pm Mon-Sat 🚌 28, 42, 59

Museu da Farmácia (5, D5)

This museum, opened in 1996, covers over 5,000 years of pharmaceutical history with artefacts from Ancient Egypt through to modern times. It's a fascinating museum with wonderfully kitsch dioramas of four entire pharmacies (the one from 19th-century Macau is the best), as well as objects such as ornate vases, bottles and pharmacy jars.

☎ 213 400 680 ✉ Rua Marechal Saldanha 1, Bica € €4/2 ✷ 10am-6pm Mon-Fri, last Sun of month 2-6pm 🚊 28 🚌 58

FREE WATERS

There are several sights in Lisbon related to the supply of fresh water to the city. Starting with the **Aqueduto das Águas Livres** (Aqueduct of Free Waters; p24), this structure was built to bring Lisbon its first clean drinking water under the orders of Dom João V. In the Praça do Príncipe Real (p28) is the **Reservatório da Patriarcal**, an underground water reservoir constructed between 1860 and 1864. Just down the road is **Enoteca Chafariz do Vinho** (p55), not where they turn water into wine, but an atmospheric restored public water reservoir. Last, but not least, is the **Museu da Água** (above), which neatly ties the whole thing together!

LISBON FOR CHILDREN

Jardim Zoológico (2, C1)
Lisbon's Zoological Garden is 'home' to a wide variety of species, with a total of over 2000 animals. The highlight for most visitors is the dolphin show and there's a cable car, rowboats, amusement park and lovely gardens.
☎ 217 232 900 ⬛ www .zoolisboa.pt ✉ Estada de Benfica 158-160, Benfica € €11/8.30 ⏲ 10am-8pm 19 Mar–18 Sep, 10am-6pm 19 Sep–19 Mar Ⓜ Jardim Zoológico 🚌 46, 58

Museu da Marioneta (5, C5)
Located in the grand old Convento das Bernardas, this puppet museum is a tidy little collection of shadow puppets (kids can try to do their own), Punch and Judy, Vietnamese water and elephant puppets, and full-sized Portuguese creations, including stages for filming puppet shows. Note that some puppets appear a little macabre to small children and jittery adults.
☎ 213 942 810 ✉ Rua da Esperança 146, Santos € €2.50/1.30.30 ⏲ 10am-1pm & 2-6pm Wed-Sun 🚊 15

Museu de Ciência (5, D4)
This interactive museum will be fascinating to any

Interactive visits at Pavilhão do Conhecimento

children with an interest in the sciences. The emphasis is on physics and the displays are entertaining and educational. There is some old scientific equipment on display, formerly used in teaching at the university, and there's also a small planetarium.
☎ 213 921 808 ⬛ www .museu-de-ciencia.ul.pt ✉ Rua da Escola Politécnica 56, Rato ⏲ 10am-1pm & 2-5pm Mon-Fri, 3-6pm Sat Ⓜ Rato, Avenida 🚌 58

Pavilhão do Conhecimento (2, F2)
Established in 1999, the Pavilion of Knowledge is an interactive museum of science and technology, located at the Parque das Nações (p19). Combined with a visit to its Oceanário de Lisboa it makes a great day out for the kids. There are 66 interactive exhibits explaining

both scientific and natural phenomena, and there's a fun playground where three- to six-year-olds can construct (or demolish!) a kid-sized house. There's also a free (but time-limited) cybercafé.
☎ 218 917 100 ⬛ www .pavconhecimento.pt ✉ Parque das Nações € adult/child 7-17/child 3-6 €6/3/2.50 ⏲ 10am-6pm Tue-Fri 11am-7pm Sat & Sun

Planetário Calouste Gulbenkian (2, A3)
Founded by the Gulbenkian Foundation, which runs the Museu Calouste Gulbenkian (p13), this planetarium is adjacent to the Museu de Marinha (p22). It offers shows in Portuguese, English and French, explaining the solar system, summer and winter sky's stars. There are also other programmes. Phone ahead for the schedule.
☎ 213 620 002 ⬛ www .planetario.online.pt ✉ Praça do Império, Belém € €4/2 ⏲ 10am-6pm Tue-Sun 🚊 15 🚌 27, 28 🚆 Belém (Cascais line)

BABY-SITTING
Most midrange and top-end hotels have access to baby-sitting services and these are the best options for short-term visitors.

Trips & Tours

WALKING TOURS
Atmospheric Alfama

Grab the No 28 tram from Rua da Conceição straight to Alfama's Largo da Graça as we're going to start high and work our way down! If you're reasonably fit, hike up to the **Miradouro da Senhora do Monte** (**1**) for spectacular views of Lisbon and the Rio Tejo (Tagus River). Walk back down to visit **Igreja de Graça** (**2**; p29) with more excellent views from **Miradouro da Graça** (**3**). Make your way down to **São Vicente de Fora** (**4**; p20) and check out the wonderful tilework and rooftop views. Take a walk along Arco Grande de Cima to Campo de Santo Clara, and if it's Tuesday or Saturday, poke around the **Feira da Ladre** (Thieves Market; **5**; p46). Head down to the **Panteão Nacional** (**6**; p17) for another wonderful vista. Walk through typically narrow, atmospheric Alfama streets to the **Largo das Portas de Sol** (**7**) for another magical view and refreshment. Check out the **Museu de Artes Decorativas** (**8**; p21) across the road before trekking up to **Castelo de São Jorge** (**9**; p8) for what many consider to be the best view of all.

Distance 3km **Duration** 3-4hr (incl museums) ▶ **Start** Largo da Graça ● **End** Castelo de São Jorge

Sunset splendour: Castelo de São Jorge (p8) at sunset

Speciality Shopping Walk

This walk takes us to some of the most unique and interesting shops in Lisbon! We start in Rossio with a visit to **Azevedo Rua** (**1**; p34), the hat shop that's been covering bald spots since 1886. Go around to Largo de

São Domingos and hit **A Ginjinha** (**2**; p62) to try yourself a kick-starting cherry brandy – if you like it, buy some! Now stroll over to **Manuel Tavares** (**3**; p45) for the tasty port and pork, then head a couple of doors further down Rua da Betesga to **Confeitaria Nacional** (**4**; p45) for some delicious pack-aged biscuits or just-right custard tarts. Head past the chestnut sell-ers (and partake if you like), up to Rua do Carmo, stopping off at **Luvaria Ulisees** (**5**; p47) for some custom, handmade gloves. Now turn right onto Rua Garrett and call into the classic **Livraria Ber-trand** (**6**; p41) to pick up a book of poetry by Pessoa (you'll need it later!). Continue awhile along Rua Garrett, then take a left down Rua do Alecrim to **Fábrica Sant'Ana** (**7**; p40) for some excellent *azulejos* (hand-painted tiles). Then, travel up and around to **Vellas Loreto** (**8**; p47), where artisans have been

Livraria Bertrand bookstore (p41)

making candles by hand since 1789. Head back to Rua Garrett and join Pessoa on a streetside table for a well-deserved *bica* (short black) at **Café A Brasilia** (**9**; p59).

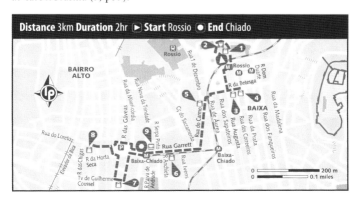

Distance 3km **Duration** 2hr ▶ **Start** Rossio ● **End** Chiado

Belém's Best

This tour guides you through the pick of Belém's best sights, starting at the watchtower, **Torre de Belém** (**1**; p26). Enjoy its whimsical, flamboyant style, then go for a walk through the garden. Head back onto the waterfront, where the **Padrão dos Descobrimentos** (**2**; p26) is framed by the Ponte 25 de Abril in the background. After taking in the view from the monument, make your way under Avenida da Índia and head to the **Centro Cultural de Belém** (**3**; p21) to check out the very cool **Museu do Design** (**4**; p22). Pass Praça do Imperio for some learning at the **Museu de Marinha** (**5**; p22) and the **Museu Nacional de Arqueologia** (**6**; p23). Now, saving the best for last, make your way to the extravagant **Mosteiro dos Jerónimos** (**7**; p10). Cross over Largo dos Jerónimos and head down Rua de Belém on to the street parallel, Rua Vieira Portuense. Unwind and enjoy a long lunch at one of the restaurants that line the street. Save room for dessert and head back to Rua Belém to **Pastéis de Belém** (**8**; p60) for their tempting trademark *pastéis de Belém* (custard tarts). Refuelled, keep heading down Rua de Belém for something just as rich, the **Museu Nacional dos Coches** (**9**; p23).

Museu do Design (p22)

Distance 3km **Duration** at least a half day (incl museums)
▶ **Start** Torre de Belém   ● **End** Museu Nacional dos Coches

DAY TRIPS
Cascais & Estoril (1, A2)

Ever since the royal family spent their first summer at the fishing village of Cascais (kush-*kaish*) way back in 1870, Lisboetas have been flocking to this pretty seaside town, with its pastel-painted houses, for sun and surf. Now a sophisticated resort destination, Cascais has an attractive old town, fine museums and a beautiful park. Also worth a peek is the whimsical, Moorish-inspired 19th-century mansion, **Museu Condes de Castro Guimarães** (☎ 214 825 407; €1.60; ☼ 11am-5pm Tue-Sun), with half-hourly guided tours. Its exotic interior is filled with a collection of Oriental carpets, 17th-century Indo-Portuguese inlaid furniture and wonderful *azulejos*. The atmospheric back streets of the old town definitely deserve exploring, but it's the beach that most people come for. Praia do Guincho, in particular, is excellent for swimming and surfing.

INFORMATION
28km northwest of Lisbon

- 🚇 Cais do Sodré to Cascais via Estoril (30min)
- 🖳 www.estorilcoast-tourism.com
- ℹ️ tourist office Cascais (☎ 214 868 204; Rua Visconde da Luz 14)
- 🚖 Apeadeiro (☎ 214 832 731; Avenida Vasco da Gama 252, Cascais)

Take a walk 2km east along the waterfront path and you'll arrive at elegant Estoril (shtoe-*reel*). Long considered Lisbon's Riviera, it was a popular destination for exiles (and spies!) flocking to neutral Portugal during WWII. They came for its tranquility and its gambling. Estoril's **casino** was once Europe's grandest and provided the inspiration for Ian Fleming's *Casino Royale*. Estoril's pretty palm tree–lined **Praia de Tamariz** attracts quite a mixed crowd these days. You'll find plenty of wealthy retirees and a bevvy of beautiful young Lisboetas staying slim in the saltwater swimming pool and basking by the beachside bars and cafés.

Riding a wave at Praia do Guincho, Cascais

Sintra (1, A1)

In the cool, hilly woodlands of the Serra de Sintra, fairytale Sintra, with its spellbinding palaces and tranquil walks, was once a popular vacation spot for Portugal's nobility. Historically fascinating – the Iberians worshipped cults here, the Moors built a castle, and after the 1755 earthquake Portugal's royals sought refuge here – Sintra's centre is now a Unesco World Heritage site.

The enchanting 13th-century **Palácio Nacional de Sintra** (Sintra National Palace; ☎ 219 053 340; Largo Rainha Dona Amélia; €3/free; ⏰ 10am-5pm Thu-Mon), with its two enormous conical chimneys, has a marvellous collection of 15th- and 16th-century *azulejos*. Repeatedly redecorated over the centuries, it's now a fascinating combination of three different residences, decorated in an amalgamation of styles and influences.

INFORMATION

28km northwest of Lisbon

- 🚆 Entrecampos station to Sintra (45min)
- 💻 www.cm-sintra.pt
- € Palácio Nacional de Sintra €3/1.50
- ℹ️ tourist office (☎ 219 231 157; Praça da República 23)
- 🍴 Toco do Javali (☎ 219 233 503; Rua 1 de Dezembro, São Pedro)

Magical, Bavarian-Manueline **Palácio Nacional da Pena** (Pena National Palace; ⏰ 219 105 340; €3.50/2, incl Parque da Pena €6/4; ⏰ 10am-5pm) is much photographed because of its turrets and battlements, coloured in kitsch lemon, lavender and rose. Yet its eccentric interior, crammed with extraordinary treasures, is just as intriguing. Parque da Pena, with its lakes, woodlands and exotic foliage, is also worth a ramble.

On the mountainside above Sintra, the Moorish ruins of **Castelo dos Mouros** (☎ 219 107 970; €3.50/2; ⏰ 9am-6pm, 7pm or 8pm depending on time of year) with its crumbling battlements, offer sublime views over Sintra and its surroundings. The exhilarating 4km walk, partly through the woods, is wonderfully peaceful.

World heritage Palácio Nacional de Sintra

See the Alfama sights in style: join a tram tour

ORGANISED TOURS

Carristur (6, C5)

Lisbon's transport company offers numerous tours of the city. The Discoveries Tour and the enigmatically named Hills Tramcar take tram routes 15 and 28 respectively, with recorded or live commentary. The Olisipo and Tagus Tours are in open-top, double-decker buses and include commentary. You can get on or off at any stop during the day, with the Olisipo Tour going up to Parque das Nações and back through the Bairro Alto, while the 'Tagus' tour takes in Amoreiras and Belém.

☎ 213 582 334 ▯ www .carristur.pt ✉ Praça do Comércio, Baixa € Discoveries or Hills Tramcar €17/8, Olisipo or Tagus €14/7 ☾ 9am-8pm Ⓜ Baixa-Chiado ⊡ 15, 18 ⊟ 9, 36, 45, 46, 59, 91

Cityline

These open-bus tours are of the hop-on-hop-off variety, with convenient stops on the circular route such as Belém, Docas and Estrela. Buses run hourly or half-hourly depending on the season.

☎ 213 191 090, 213 864 322 ▯ www.cityline -sightline.pt € €15, child up to 5 free ☾ 9am-6pm (buses every 30min) Apr-Oct, 10am-5pm (buses hourly) Nov-Mar

Cityrama (5, C1)

Cityrama runs sightseeing bus tours of Lisbon and surrounding regions, including a five-hour city tour, Lisbon by Night. This evening tour will introduce you to the celebrated *fado* tradition. Other tours encompass Lisbon plus Sintra and the Estoril coast. While they all depart from Parque Eduardo VII, there is pick-up service from selected hotels.

☎ 213 191 091 ▯ www .cityrama.pt ✉ Parque Eduardo VII ☾ day tours leave at 9am, Lisbon by Night 8pm € City Tour €31, Full Day Tour €71, Lisbon by Night with/without dinner €74.50/61 Ⓜ Marquês de Pombal

Inside Tours (6, B2)

Inside Tours provides two English-language walking tours in Lisbon. The first is a three-hour morning tour of the main sights. The second tour is more of a crawl than a walk – yes, a pub crawl! With a nip of *ginjinha* (see p62) to get the tour started, you're off to Chiado and then the Bairro Alto on a four-hour bar hop. No bookings required, just turn up at the meeting point in front of Rossio train station.

☎ 217 933 511 € walking tour €18/15, pub crawl incl some drinks €15 ☾ walking tour at 9.30am, pub crawl at 9pm Ⓜ Restauradores

Transtejo (5, F6)

These 2½-hour multilingual Rio Tejo boat cruises run from April to October and head to Parque das Nações, then Belém.

☎ 218 820 348/9 ▯ www .transtejo.pt ✉ Terreiro do Paço Terminal € €20/8 ☾ 3pm Ⓜ Baixa-Chiado ⊡ 15, 18 ⊟ 9, 36, 45, 46, 59, 91

Shopping

Lisbon is such a fabulous place to shop, with one fine, handmade leather shoe firmly in the past and one colourful funky sneaker kickin' it into the future.

The Baixa and Chiado have those wonderfully charming 'olde worlde' and often eccentric specialist stores run by the same master-craftspeople who've run them for centuries, passing their techniques from generation to generation. They're the kind of stores your grandmother used to take you to – a store for hats, a store for gloves, a store for buttons, a store for tinned tuna and so on. The Bairro Alto, on the other hand, is at the opposite end of the spectrum, with its steep, narrow streets full of cutting-edge young designers pushing fashion to the limits. Here you will find their cool street wear and club gear, innovative jewellery, hip accessories, stylish design products, with DJs in every store. You'll also be able to lay your hands on everything else in between – you know, the kind of shopping you can find in nearly every other city around the world – the brand names, luxury franchises and shopping malls. But why would you want to shop at these soulless places when Lisbon offers you the best of both shopping worlds, past and future, in its own delightfully idiosyncratic style?

Both old and new create Lisbon's fashion

The shopping experience in Lisbon is so pleasurable because the pace is relaxed. Unlike in London or Paris, nobody is rushing madly anywhere at anytime, except perhaps when they're picking up something after work on their way home. Prices are still some of the lowest in Europe, and during the summer sales many offer discounts of up to 50%. During August, many shops take a break *para férias* (for holidays) for a week or so. Shopaholics should get the Lisboa Shopping Card, which gets you discounts of up to 20% in over 200 selected stores, and is available at Turismos de Lisboa.

OPENING TIMES
Most city-centre shops open from 9am to 1pm and then from 3pm to 7pm on weekdays, and close at 1pm on Saturday, while stores in shopping malls stay open as late as 10pm everyday. Bairro Alto boutiques open late afternoon and often don't shut until midnight. Most shops close on Sunday and public holidays, such as Easter, Christmas and New Year's Day.

ANTIQUES & CRAFTS

Antiquália (6, A4)
Right in the heart of Chiado, Antiquália offers a tempting array of fine antiques and collectables. Gorgeous furniture, chandeliers and decorative arts dating from the 18th century onwards are spread throughout several rooms.

☎ 213 423 260 ✉ Praça Luís de Camões 37, Chiado ⏲ 10am-7pm Mon-Fri, 10am-1.30pm Sat Ⓜ Baixa-Chiado 🚋 28

Arte Rústica (6, C3)
This shop stocks an eclectic collection of hand-painted ceramics, hand-embroidered tablecloths (mainly from Madeira) and other Portuguese handicrafts. Rustica makes a great one-stop-shop if you're not an all-day shopper. It also stocks Lisbon T-shirts and other souvenirs.

☎ 213 421 127 ✉ Rua d'Aurea 246, Baixa ⏲ 9am-1pm & 3-7pm Ⓜ Baixa-Chiado 🚋 28

Donna Taraja (5, C4)
There are quite a few antique places spread along Rua de São Bento but this is the best place to start. Quality pieces and paintings from the late 18th century to the early 20th century are on offer and if you're lucky you might just find a gorgeous Art Deco piece to challenge that baggage allowance.

☎ 213 955 844 ✉ Rua de São Bento, Rato ⏲ 10am-7pm Mon-Fri, 10am-1.30pm Sat Ⓜ Rato

Azulejos at Fábrica Sant'Ana

Fábrica Sant'Ana (6, A4)
Since 1741 this tile-maker has been creating everything from tiny handmade tiles *(azulejos)* to fountains. The shop is jam-packed with a huge array of tiles (and some very cute cherubs) and while there is plenty of stuff that falls on the wrong side of kitsch, you can order wonderful custom tiles and have them shipped on to wherever you like.

☎ 213 422 537 ✉ Rua do Alecrim 95, Chiado ⏲ 9am-7pm Mon-Fri, 10am-2pm Sat Ⓜ Baixa-Chiado 🚋 28

Loja do Mundo Rural (5, B4)
While this shop is a little off the tourist trail, it makes up for it with high-quality handicrafts, such as ceramics, embroidery and tiles. There's also a *charcutaria* (delicatessen) with quite a decent selection of hams, cheeses and wines, making it a great excursion for self-catering if you also visit the nearby Campo De Ourique Mercado (p46).

☎ 213 953 889 ✉ Rua Saraiva de Carvalho 115, Campo de Ourique ⏲ 10am-8pm Mon-Sat 🚋 28 🚌 9

Madeira House (6, C4)
Ignore the gaudy souvenirs and bizarre cork products. This is the best place to buy quality hand-embroidered Madeira lace and linen, including tablecloths, placemat and napkin sets, along with colourful Barcelos' roosters and beautifully glazed Hispano-Arab geometric patterned tiles – they make great 'features' for fans of minimalism.

☎ 213 431 454 ✉ Rua Augusta 133, Baixa ⏲ 10am-8pm Mon-Fri, 9am-1pm Sat Ⓜ Baixa-Chiado 🚋 28

Vista Alegre (6, B4)
Producing fine tableware since 1824, Vista Alegre is one of the highest-quality manufacturers in the world, creating everything from the flowery Algarve setting to the understated Spirit White collection. Besides its fine porcelain plate sets, it also stocks exquisite Atlantis lead crystal, with beautiful decanters and wine-glass sets. There are also a number of stores around the city.

☎ 213 461 401 ✉ Largo do Chiado 20-23, Chiado ⏲ 10am-8pm Mon-Sat Ⓜ Baixa-Chiado 🚋 28

BOOKS & MUSIC

Discoteca Amália (6, C3)
Here is the place to come for your souvenir music – this little shop is a shrine to the late, lamented queen of *fado,* Amália Rodrigues. Besides myriad releases by the aforementioned artist, the Discoteca stocks a tidy collection of other *fado* artists, along with classical and traditional Portuguese music.
☎ 213 421 485 ⊠ Rua de Áurea 272, Baixa 🕑 10am-8pm Mon-Sat Ⓜ Baixa-Chiado 🚋 28

Discoteca Amalia for all things *fado*

Fnac (6, C4)
This store has an excellent selection of translated Portuguese literature, as well as a vast array of music, including decent *fado,* local pop and indie releases. There's a very good selection of computer and digital camera accessories for the travelling tech-head, a popular café with frequent readings and performances, and a concert box office. There's also another branch at Centro Comercial Colombo (p42).
☎ 213 221 800 ⊠ Rua Nova do Almada 110, Chiado 🕑 10am-8pm Ⓜ Baixa-Chiado 🚋 28

Livraria Bertrand (6, B4)
Trading from behind its blue-tiled façade, this is one of Lisbon's oldest bookstores. It's also the city's biggest seller of books in English, French and German, plus a range of kids titles in English and Portuguese. All the magazines and English-language titles are at the rear of the store.
☎ 213 421 941 ⊠ Rua Garrett 73, Chiado 🕑 10am-8pm Ⓜ Baixa-Chiado 🚋 28

Livraria Buchholz (5, D2)
The atmospheric old bookshop of Buchholz has a huge literature collection in the Portuguese, English, French and German languages. There's also some decent architecture books on Portugal, but unless you *fala* (speak) Portuguese, you'll just be looking at the pictures.
☎ 213 170 580 ⊠ Rua Duque de Palmela 4, Marquês de Pombal 🕑 9am-7pm Mon-Fri, 9am-1pm Sat Ⓜ Marquês de Pombal

TOP FIVE SOUNDS

- *Art of Amália* (Amália Rodrigues) The undisputed queen of *fado* at her melancholic best.
- *Fado em Mim* (Mariza) Fantastic debut album of the only *fado* singer to seriously size up Amália's throne.
- *Que Falta Você Me Faz: Músicas de Vinicius de Moraes* (Maria Bethânia) There's a reason Lisboetas say the best jazz comes from Brazil; put this CD on and see why...
- *Dead Combo Volume 1* (Dead Combo) Twangy surf noir straight from the Bairro Alto.
- *Film* (The Gift) One-part Portishead, one-part Massive Attack, overlaid with Sonia Tavares' unique voice.

TOP FIVE BOOKS
- *The Maias* (Eça de Queiroz; 1888) A poignant picture of 19th-century Lisbon.
- *The Book of Disquiet* (Fernando Pessoa; 2002) The beautiful melancholy of a Lisboan bookkeeper.
- *The Anarchist Banker* (Eugénio Lisboa, ed; 1997) Short stories by the big names in 19th- and 20th-century fiction.
- *A Small Death in Lisbon* (Robert Wilson; 1999) Portrait of Lisbon after the Revolution of the Carnations.
- *The History of the Siege of Lisbon* (José Saramago; 2000) How Lisbon's history was rewritten with a single word!

DEPARTMENT STORES & MALLS

Armazéns do Chiado
(6, C4)
After being destroyed by fire in 1988, this and the adjacent Edifício Grandela were redesigned by highly regarded Álvaro Siza Vieira, to great effect. Even greater has been how popular Armazéns do Chiado has become as a meeting point for young Lisboetas who head to Fnac (p41) or one of the restaurants on the top floor.
☎ 213 210 600 ✉ Rua do Carmo 2, Chiado ⏲ 10am-10pm, restaurants to 11pm Ⓜ Baixa-Chiado 🚊 28

Centro Comercial Colombo (2, B1)
The Comercial Colombo mall is so enormous it's almost a day trip in itself, with over 400 shops, a food court (with all the usual fast-food suspects), a health club and a cinema complex, making it a pretty decent rainy-day option.
☎ 217 113 600 ✉ Avenida Lusíada, Benfica ⏲ 10am-midnight Ⓜ Colégio Militar/Luz

Centro Vasco da Gama
(2, F2)
One of the success stories of the post–Expo '98 boom in this part of town, this shopping complex is especially popular on weekends, when families do some serious window shopping before heading to a restaurant or the nearby Oceanário de Lisboa (p19).
☎ 218 930 601 ✉ Avenida Dom João II, Parque das Nações ⏲ 10am-midnight Ⓜ Oriente

Complexo Amoreiras
(5, B2)
Lisbon's first big shopping centre is really beginning to show its age. The complex's postmodern design has dated badly (both inside and out). However, it's still popular for its cinemas and eateries.
☎ 213 810 200 ✉ Avenida Engenheiro Duarte Pacheco, Amoreiras ⏲ 10am-midnight Ⓜ Rato 🚌 58

El Corte Inglês (2, C2)
Even those familiar with this usually-large Spanish chain will be surprised at the vast size of the Lisbon branch. It's quite a one-stop shop, with decent food, clothes, sporting goods and, of course, the obligatory cinemas.
☎ 213 711 700 ✉ Avenida António Augusto de Aguiar 31, São Sebastião ⏲ Mon-Thu 10am-10pm, Fri-Sat 10am-11.30pm Ⓜ São Sebastião

Shoopping mecca: Centro Vasco da Gama

HOMEWARES & GIFTS

Area Infinity (5, B2)
This super-stylish store stocks great furniture and home accessories, but it's the wonderful Frankincense and Myrrh candle and incense sets that we love – they make great gifts! And while it might look good at home, we don't recommend taking the Umbra green translucent domino sets to one of the local Lisbon parks for a game...
☎ 213 715 350 ⊠ Complexo Amoreiras, Avenida Engenheiro Duarte Pacheco, Amoreiras ❖ 10am-midnight Ⓜ Rato 🚌 58

Cutipol (6, A4)
If you've eaten at some of Lisbon's better establishments, no doubt you'll have been using this stunning Portuguese-designed cutlery. Designs range from traditional, such as Atlântico, to the sleek Moon, designed by the talented head of design, Jose Ribeiro.
☎ 213 225 075 ⊠ Rua do Alecrim 113-115, Chiado

Charming Rua Augusta (p29), downtown in the Baixa

❖ 10am-2pm & 3-7pm Tue-Sat Ⓜ Baixa-Chiado 🚋 28

Interna Emporio Casa (5, D4)
Check out the wonderful contemporary furniture and design objects in this lovely space. While you probably won't be taking a B&B Italia sofa for the folks back home, there are great travelling accessories to be had, such as Nava messenger bags and ingenious Lexon goodies. We love the portable golf-putting kit!
☎ 213 211 290 ⊠ Rua da Escola Politécnica 42, Príncipe Real ❖ 10.30am-7.30pm Mon-Sat, closed

Sat 2.30-3.30pm Ⓜ Rato, Avenida 🚌 58

Nosso Design (6, B4)
Stocking only contemporary Portuguese design, this groovy shop will keep design tourists happy with fabulous jewellery, glassware and lamps. While the vases by mglass are stunning, our favourite gifts from Nosso Design are the Claus Porto violet hand-made soaps, presented in their original 19th-century packaging – very Nana, but very cool!
☎ 213 258 960 ⊠ Rua Serpa Pinto 12a, Chiado ❖ 11am-8.30pm Mon-Sat Ⓜ Baixa-Chiado 🚋 28

SHOPPING AREAS
- Avenida da Liberdade (5, E3) – big names in designer clothes and shoes
- Bairro Alto (6, A3) – retro and vintage fashion, hip clothes, jewellery and accessories
- Rua Augusta & Baixa (6, C4) – brand names, luxury goods and charming specialist stores
- Rua Garrett, Chiado (6, B4) – swanky shops, designer boutiques, books and music
- Rua da Escola Politécnica (5, D3) – traditional arts and handicrafts
- São Bento (5, C4) – upmarket antiques, ceramics and glassware

Very cool: Nosso Design

CLOTHING, JEWELLERY & ACCESSORIES

Agência 117 (6, A3)

This hip '70s-style boutique stocks cute Miss Sixty stuff, cool Skunk Funk gear – check out the zip-up chocolate and orange jackets! – and groovy accessories. If you like this, drop in to Fake at No 113, also run by Lisbon fashion gurus Carlos Barroso and Anselmo Ortega.

☎ 213 461 270 ✉ Rua do Norte 117, Bairro Alto ⏱ 2pm-midnight Mon-Sat Ⓜ Baixa-Chiado 🚋 28

Ana Salazar (6, B3)

Portugal's premier women's designer (and most globally successful) more often than not works with black, charcoal, teal, grey and chocolate, with splashes of other colour. Her alluring designs exude business-meets-boho – tailored and structured yet remaining soft and feminine.

☎ 213 472 289 ✉ Rua do Carmo 87, Chiado

⏱ 10am-7pm Mon-Sat Ⓜ Baixa-Chiado 🚋 28

El Dorado (6, A3)

This very cool store stocks retro, vintage and second-hand clothes, small indie labels, big sunnies, hippie chic, clubbing gear and street wear.

☎ 213 423 935 ✉ Rua do Norte 25, Bairro Alto ⏱ 2-10pm Mon-Fri, 3-10pm Sat Ⓜ Baixa-Chiado 🚋 28

Fátima Lopes (6, A3)

After Salazar, Lopes is Lisbon's next most internationally successful designer. In her funky boutique-cum-disco, you'll find slick men's and women's fashion that is cool cutting-edge while exuding strength and elegance.

☎ 213 240 546 ✉ Rua da Atalaia 36, Bairro Alto ⏱ 10am-10pm Mon-Sat Ⓜ Baixa-Chiado 🚋 28

Foreva (2, B1)

This is one very stylish label, but not only are the shoes very cool they're also very

Funky Fátima Lopes

well made. The boots are the best! There's also a store at Armazéns do Chiado (p42).

☎ 217 166 111 ✉ Centro Comercial Colombo, Avenida Lusíada, Benfica ⏱ 10am-midnight Ⓜ Colégio Militar/Luz

Hera (2, B1)

This distinguished shoemaker sells beautiful, locally designed and well-made shoes and a great range of knee-high boots, some almost bordering on cowboy-boot territory. The kids' lace-up

CLOTHING & SHOE SIZES

Women's Clothing

Aust/UK	8	10	12	14	16	18
Europe	36	38	40	42	44	46
Japan	5	7	9	11	13	15
USA	6	8	10	12	14	16

Women's Shoes

Aust/USA	5	6	7	8	9	10
Europe	35	36	37	38	39	40
France only	35	36	38	39	40	42
Japan	22	23	24	25	26	27
UK	3½	4½	5½	6½	7½	8½

Men's Clothing

Aust	92	96	100	104	108	112
Europe	46	48	50	52	54	56
Japan	S	M	M		L	
UK/USA	35	36	37	38	39	40

Men's Shirts (Collar Sizes)

Aust/Japan	38	39	40	41	42	43
Europe	38	39	40	41	42	43
UK/USA	15	15½	16	16½	17	17½

Men's Shoes

Aust/UK	7	8	9	10	11	12
Europe	41	42	43	44½	46	47
Japan	26	27	27.5	28	29	30
USA	7½	8½	9½	10½	11½	12½

Measurements approximate only; try before you buy.

shoes are very cute. Also at Complexo Amoreiras (p42).
☎ 217 168 400 ✉ Centro Comercial Colombo, Avenida Lusíada, Benfica ⏲ 10am-midnight Ⓜ Colégio Militar/Luz

Lena Aires (6, A3)
One of Lisbon's leading designers specialises in up-to-the-minute hipness but in her own original style. Lena Aires' gear is edgy yet feminine, and often glamorous.
☎ 213 461 815 ✉ Rua da Atalaia 96, Bairro Alto ⏲ 1-8pm Mon-Wed, 1-10pm Thu-Sat Ⓜ Baixa-Chiado 🚊 28

Sneakers Delight (6, A3)
Here, sneakers are objets d'art. Both store branches resemble avant-garde art galleries over retail outlets. The modish branch at Santa Apolónia (☎ 213 478 821; Ave Infante Dom Henrique) has a hair stylist, Facto-Lab.
☎ 213 479 976 ✉ Rua do Norte 30-32, Bairro Alto ⏲ 1-11pm Mon-Sat Ⓜ Baixa-Chiado 🚊 28

Zara (6, C4)
Zara's is catwalk-inspired Iberian fashion – whatever you like on the Paris or Milan runways, you're guaranteed to find a funky variation at a fraction of the price here a few weeks later. There's too cool casual, evening and work clothes, plus funky shoes, handbags, belts, bikinis and lingerie, as well as men's and kids' sections.
☎ 213 241 400, 213 243 720 ✉ Rua Augusta 71-81 & 157-171, Baixa ⏲ 9.30am-7.30pm Mon-Sat Ⓜ Rossio, Baixa-Chiado 🚊 28

PORT FOR A STORM

While port is one of the most famous exports of Portugal, it isn't as popular a drink as you would expect. Originally a happy (and potent) accident from adding brandy to Portuguese wines to preserve them during long boat trips to England in the 1700s, by the 1800s this fortified wine had really developed into something special.

Today the strictly controlled production of port is great for consumers. If shopping for port, here are the very best vintages of the last century and what to do with them: 1912, 1937 and 1945, drink now; 1963 and 1970, drink or cellar; 1884, 1994 and 2000, cellar. And don't be fooled by the colour of port – it actually gets lighter as it ages…

FOOD & DRINK

Casa Macário (6, C3)
This alluring little shop, dating from 1913, specialises in ports and wines, coffee and confectionery. Wines thoughtfully have descriptions in English and French, wine racks are labelled 'don't clean the bottles', and there's some decent vintage port here too.
☎ 213 420 900 ✉ Rua Augusta 272, Baixa ⏲ 9am-7pm Mon-Sat Ⓜ Rossio, Baixa-Chiado 🚊 15, 28

Charcutaria Brasil (5, D3)
Every neighbourhood should have this kind of delicatessen, with shelves stacked to the ceiling that make browsing endlessly fascinating. There's always something freshly cooked (such as aromatic spit-roasted chickens) making great takeaway, there are some great old ports on the shelves (some Porto Barros 1935 vintage), and the sausages, hams and cheeses are mouth-wateringly good.
☎ 213 885 644 ✉ Rua Alexandre Herculano 90, Rato ⏲ 8am-9pm Mon-Fri, 8am-2pm Sat Ⓜ Rato

Confeitaria Nacional (6, C3)
This quaint old *confeitaria* (a shop that sells sweets or pastries), founded in 1829, is a great spot to drop in for a quick *café pingado* (espresso with a little milk) and pick up some of the wonderfully packaged biscuits that make a great gift – if you can stop yourself from eating them…
☎ 213 461 720 ✉ Praça da Figueira 18B-C, Rossio ⏲ 8am-8pm Mon-Fri, 8am-2pm Sat Ⓜ Rossio, Baixa-Chiado 🚊 28

Manuel Tavares (6, C3)
The window display of this lovely Art Deco shop is jam-packed with wine, port and delicatessen items. Inside you'll find a bewildering array of ports, but what we love here is the *morcelas* (blood sausage) and the range of other *chouriços* (sausages) that make a great snack with some of the wonderful cheeses on offer.
☎ 213 424 209 ✉ Rua da Betesga 1A-B, Baixa ⏲ Mon-Sat 9am-7.30pm Ⓜ Rossio, Baixa-Chiado 🚊 28

BUY LISBON

The best buys in Lisbon are uniquely Portuguese products. Here's what to buy and where to find it:

- *Azulejos* (ceramic tiles) – Fábrica Sant'Ana (p40)
- Madeira lace and linen – Madeira House (p40)
- Lisboan haute couture – Ana Salazar (p44)
- *Fado* music – Discoteca Amália (p41)
- Port wine – Napoleão (below)
- Pork sausage – Manuel Tavares (p45)
- *Pastéis de nata* (custard tarts) – Confeitaria Nacional (p45)

Napoleão (6, D4)
For us, this is *the* shop for port lovers. The staff is knowledgeable, the selection is excellent and you can even have a little tipple on the house. The '100 years of Port' collection makes a great gift; it's a small set of Presidential Porto ports that are 10, 20, 30 and 40 years old. The staff knows their Portuguese wines equally as well.
☎ 218 861 108 ✉ Rua dos Franqueiros 70, Baixa 🕒 9am-8pm Mon-Sat 🚇 Baixa-Chiado 🚋 28

Vini Portugal (6, C5)
This stylish showroom for Portuguese wines offers information on the wine regions of Portugal as well as offering a rotating roster of wines to taste and buy.
☎ 213 420 690 ✉ Lisboa Welcome Center, Praça do Comércio, Baixa 🕒 10am-6pm Tue-Sat 🚇 Baixa-Chiado

FOR CHILDREN

Bon Point (6, B4)
This Paris-based brand serves up some beautifully made classic and funky clothing for kids aged zero to 16, from its only Portuguese outlet. We love the winter range; especially cute are the pullovers (with mittens attached!) and for the older kids the girls range is outstanding.
☎ 213 476 650 ✉ Rua Ivens 15A, Chiado 🕒 10am-7pm Mon-Fri, 10am-6pm Sat 🚇 Baixa-Chiado 🚋 28

Du Pareil au Même (6, B4)
A great place to get those practical baby travel accessories (for bottle feeding, baby carrying) and if your stroller comes out the loser in its battle with Lisbon's cobblestones, it stocks Maclaren strollers. There's a good range of clothes for kids aged from zero to 14.
☎ 213 259 751 ✉ Rua Garett 82-86, Chiado 🕒 10am-7pm Mon-Sat 🚇 Baixa-Chiado 🚋 28

Papo d'Anjo (6, B4)
This Lisbon-based children's wear company generally uses 100% cotton or wool for its classic lines of boys' and girls' clothing, which covers the zero-to-12-years-old age group. The A-line dresses for girls are the most popular item and the boy's Classic pants are well made and hard wearing. The baby baskets (in pink or blue, of course!) make the perfect newborn gift.
☎ 213 420 337 ✉ Rua Ivens 8, Chiado 🕒 10am-7pm Mon-Fri, 10am-6pm Sat 🚇 Baixa-Chiado 🚋 28

MARKETS

Campo De Ourique Mercado (5, A4)
A great little local market that's worth visiting from Tuesday to Saturday when locals crowd around early to get the best fish. There's also a decent *bacalhau* (salted cod) shop and some fantastic regional cheeses as well. Combine your trip here with a visit to the Loja do Mundo Rural (p40).
✉ cnr Rua Padre Francisco & Rua Coelho da Rocha, Campo de Ourique 🕒 7am-2pm Mon-Sat 🚋 28 🚌 9

Feira da Ladra (4, C1)
A motley collection of Lisboetas and their equally eclectic wares spread out virtually all the way from the Mosteiro de São Vicente de Fora (p20) to the Panteão Nacional de Santa Engrácia (p17) for Lisbon's best-known flea market (its name means

'thieves market'). You'll find everything from army surplus gear and ramshackle CD collections to incense and piles of clothes. And that's just one stall…

✉ São Vicente, Campo de Santa Clara, Graça ⏲ 8am-1pm Tue, until around 5pm Sat 🚃 28

Mercado da Ribeira
(6, A5)
Even if you're not doing a spot of self-catering, this market provides great entertainment as the stallholders are as interesting as the fresh produce. Arrive early if you actually want to buy, as shoppers get here early. Every Sunday the marketplace is taken over by the **Feira de Coleccionismo** (Collectors' Market; ⏲ 9am-1pm). The name is code for stamp, coins and collectable-card geeks.

☎ 210 312 600 ✉ Avenida 24 de Julho, Cais do Sodré station ⏲ 6am-2pm Mon-Sat Ⓜ Cais do Sodré

Conserveira de Lisboa

TOP FIVE BIZARRE SOUVENIRS
- Candles shaped (and smelling) like vegetables (Vellas Loreto, below)
- The Barcelos' Rooster (Madeira House, p40)
- Canned fish (Conserveira de Lisboa, below)
- Cork wallets and purses (Madeira House, p40)
- 100 years of Port (Napoleão, p46)

SPECIALIST STORES

Azevedo Rua (6, C2)
This wonderful hat shop has been around since 1886 and it doesn't look like the styles in the display cases have changed a bit – that's fine by us, as fashion comes and goes anyway, so you're always bound to find something here that's 'in'. There's a great range on offer – berets, Panama hats, bonnets and bowlers – and should you choose to wear such things, this is your only destination in Lisbon for top hats.

☎ 213 427 511 ✉ Praça Dom Pedro IV 72-73, Baixa ⏲ 9am-7pm Mon-Fri, 9am-1pm Sat Ⓜ Rossio, Baixa-Chiado 🚃 28

Conserveira de Lisboa
(6, D4)
Fittingly located in the street of the 'cod boats', the little retro-tastic Conserveira de Lisboa shop stocks tinned fish – and we mean virtually nothing but tinned fish. Design buffs will love the packaging, foodies will love the taste (get the ones with peppers) and everyone will love the two old ladies who run the place.

☎ 218 871 058 ✉ Rua dos Bacalhoeiros 34, Baixa ⏲ 9.30am-7pm Mon-Sat Ⓜ Baixa-Chiado 🚃 28, 15

Luvaria Ulisees (6, B3)
Perhaps no other shop represents Lisbon charm better than this petite specialist handmade-glove store. Choose your style and colour, return 24 hours later and your custom gloves will be expertly fitted to your hand in store. They can produce everything from ¾-length women's silk gloves (think Audrey Hepburn in *Breakfast at Tiffany's*) to beautiful little kid-leather ones, and gentlemen aren't left out – they do excellent driving gloves.

☎ 213 420295, Rua do Carmo 87A, Baixa ⏲ 9.30am-7pm Mon-Sat Ⓜ Baixa-Chiado

Vellas Loreto (6, A4)
This wonderful little candle shop has been around since 1789 and the candles are still handmade by the family from an original formula. This doesn't mean that they're not experimenting – the latest range includes scents such as green tea, honey, and our favourite, tomato-leaf fragrance. Last time we visited the window display was a (knowingly) kitschy set of vegetable-shaped candles…

☎ 213 425 387 ✉ Rua do Loreto 53, Bairro Alto ⏲ 9am-7pm Mon-Fri, 9am-1pm Sat Ⓜ Baixa-Chiado 🚃 28

Eating

An outside table on an enigmatic cobblestone street. The smell of fragrant, fresh grilled sardines fills the air, crisp white wine sits chilled on the table where flavoursome cheese and strong *chouriço* sausage tempt your tastebuds. This is Lisbon dining at its best. The only thing that can possibly fracture this picture is that after the first few of these typically Lisboan meals you might start to wonder, well, is there more?

There's a reason that most Lisboetas, when going to their favourite restaurant, don't need to see the menu – it probably hasn't changed in 30 years. But as younger Lisboetas travel more, or live outside Portugal, they return wondering if there's more as well. So in recent years the dining scene in Lisbon has seen some restaurateurs and chefs start to take liberties with traditional Portuguese fare, and while *bacalhau* (dried, salted cod) and *açorda* (bread soup) will still feature on these menus, you can expect to see them handled innovatively. However, there is something reassuring about returning to your favourite restaurant after a couple of years' absence and finding that it's not now doing Modern British and Pacific Rim on the one menu…

Breakfast in Lisbon is the classic European tradition of a pastry and a strong coffee, usually taken standing up at the bar of a favoured *pastelaria* (pastry shop). Lunch, usually taken between 1pm and 3pm, is a hearty affair of three courses and copious amounts of wine that leave visitors wondering how anything gets done when locals return to work! Dinner is usually more of the same, but Lisboetas may not have dinner until 10pm, although restaurants are usually busy with tourists from 7.30pm. Most restaurants listed in this chapter are family-friendly and restaurants will be quite used to whipping up something different for the kids.

MEAL COSTS

The pricing symbols used in this chapter indicate the cost of a two-course meal (starter and main) for one person, excluding drinks. One thing to note about Lisbon meals is that those cheeses, olives and other delectable snacks that arrive at the table are not included in the meal prices and while you generally won't be charged if you don't snack on them, it's worth checking the bill to make sure.

€€€€	over €40
€€€	€26-40
€€	€16-25
€	under €15

ROSSIO, PRAÇA DOS RESTAURADORES & BAIXA

Andorra (6, B2)
Portuguese €€
For a seafood lunch in the sun-filled city centre, Andorra makes for a great stop. Order some charcoal-grilled sardines or a more filling *arroz de marisco* (seafood casserole) and some white wine from the easy-going staff, and do some people watching.
☎ 213 426 047
✉ Rua das Portas de Santo Antão 82 ⏲ noon-midnight
Ⓜ Restauradores

Bonjardim (6, B2)
Portuguese €€
If you're wondering why people make a fuss about Portuguese chicken, this casual eatery is the place to answer your question. Here the charcoal-roasted birds are brilliant, moist and succulent, and while we love them with *piri-piri* (a hot chilli sauce), some don't like it hot.
☎ 213 424 389 ✉ Travessa de Santo Antão 11 ⏲ noon-11pm Ⓜ Restauradores

Café Martinho da Arcada (6, C4)
Portuguese €€
This wonderful old café-restaurant, set in the arcades of Praça do Comércio and dating back to 1782, makes a great choice for an outdoor lunch. Regional Portuguese specialities such as *cataplana de peixes mistos* (fish stew) are excellent and it's also a great place to drop in for a

BUSINESS DINING
Lisbon has many more romantic restaurants than great business ones, but here are a few restaurants guaranteed to keep clients happy:
- Eleven (p55)
- Flores (p51)
- Ristorant Hotel Cipriani (p57)
- Bica do Sapato (p52)
- Terreiro do Paço (p50)

quick coffee and a *pastéis de nata* (custard tart).
☎ 218 879 259 ✉ Praça do Comércio 3 ⏲ 7am-11pm Mon-Sat Ⓜ Baixa-Chiado

Cais da Ribeira (6, A6)
Portuguese €€€€
Located next to the ferry terminal and with wonderful views of El Tejo, this cosy eatery, not surprisingly, specialises in fresh seafood. The simply grilled fresh fish is always wonderful and the paella is a house speciality.
☎ 213 423 611 ✉ Rua da Cintura, Armazém A-2 ⏲ 7.30-11.30pm Tue, 7.30pm-2am Wed-Sat, noon-4pm & 7-11pm Sun Ⓜ Cais do Sodré

Gambrinus (6, C2)
Seafood €€€€
With its dark wood-panelled dining rooms, renowned Gambrinus sets a very different tone from the other seafood restaurants along this busy eat street. It's also

set apart by the quality of its seafood (listen to the daily specials) and cooking that's far more sophisticated. With oysters, caviar and lobster all big movers, it's a great restaurant for a decadent seafood feast.
☎ 213 421 466 ✉ Rua Portas de Santo Antão 23-25 ⏲ noon-2am Ⓜ Restauradores

Solmar (6, B1)
Seafood €€€
With its vast undersea mosaic and lobster tanks, it is clear what's on offer at this busy seafood restaurant and café. Once a firm favourite for a Lisbon seafood feast, it doesn't appear to attract the same clientele as it used to, but thankfully the *açorda de mariscos* (bread soup with seafood) hasn't changed a bit.
☎ 213 460 010 ✉ Rua Portas de Santo Antão 106 ⏲ noon-midnight Ⓜ Restauradores

Seafood feast: the colourful Solmar (p49)

Terreiro do Paço (6, C5)
Modern Portuguese €€€
Designed as a showcase of Portuguese gastronomy, this wonderful restaurant fills its brief with fantastic produce and skilful, imaginative cooking, matched with excellent Portuguese wine – Vini Portugal (p46) is next door. It's a restaurant that every Lisbon restaurateur should take a notebook to. During summer you can dine in the shade of the colonnaded arcades, but we love the upstairs dining room with its exposed brickwork.
☎ 210 312 850 ⊠ Lisboa Welcome Center, Praça do Comércio ⏲ 12.30-3.30pm & 8-11pm Tue-Sat, 12.30-3.30pm Mon
Ⓜ Baixa-Chiado

BAIRRO ALTO & CHIADO

O Barrigas (6, A3)
Portuguese €€
This inviting little *adega* (bar-restaurant) serves up some classic Portuguese seafood dishes such as *bacalhau espiritual* (like a soufflé) as well as meat and vegetarian options. Makes for a decent, filling, pre-Bairro bar-hop stop – the name means 'the

Classic Portuguese fare: Bota Alta

bellies', which is what you'll need to work off after eating here!
☎ 213 471 220 ⊠ Travessa da Queimada 31 ⏲ 7pm-2am Ⓜ Baixa-Chiado
🚋 28 Ⓥ

Bota Alta (6, A3)
Portuguese €€
This classic, crowded eatery satisfies faithful diners with its old-school Portuguese dishes – perfect fodder for lining your stomach before hitting the bars. The house wine's very drinkable and this is a great place to try some *bacalhau* – check what's on the specials menu.
☎ 213 427 959 ⊠ Travessa da Queimada 37 ⏲ noon-2.30pm & 7-10.30pm
Ⓜ Baixa-Chiado 🚋 28

Brasserie de L'Entrecôte (6, A4)
Brasserie €€€
This is Lisbon's best version of the classic French brasserie, serving up decent slabs of free-range beef in a convincingly authentic setting. This being Portugal, of course, the portions are heart-cloggingly huge, but punters who can make

it on to dessert are richly rewarded.

☎ 213 473 616
✉ Rua do Alecrim 117, Chiado ⏲ 12.30-4pm & 8pm-midnight
Ⓜ Baixa-Chiado 🚋 28

Brasuca (5, D5)
Brazilian €€
Brasuca has been a bastion of Brazilian cooking in Lisbon for a couple of decades. Eating at this place is more akin to attending a dinner party than a restaurant thanks to its cosy atmosphere and hearty cooking. Try the classic *feijoada* (meat, black bean and rice stew) or one of the excellent cod-based dishes, washed down with a *caipirinha* (cocktail) .
☎ 213 220 740 ✉ Rua João Pereira da Rosa 7 ⏲ Tue-Sun noon-3pm & 7-11pm 🚋 28

Calcuta (6, A3)
Indian €
Busy for both lunch and dinner, this authentic eatery serves up tasty northern Indian fare. Anything from the tandoori oven is recommended (try the breads) and there are some good vegetarian choices. Great before heading out in the Bairro Alto.
☎ 213 428 295 ✉ Rua do Norte 17 ⏲ noon-3pm & 6.30-11pm Mon-Fri, 6.30-11pm Sat Ⓜ Baixa-Chiado 🚋 28 Ⓥ

Casa Nostra (6, A3)
Italian €€€
This stylishly understated eatery is one of the best Italian restaurants in town. The pastas are made fresh, the risottos are cooked to perfection, and if you don't

ROOMS WITH A VIEW
Lisbon has several restaurants offering water views or interesting city vistas.
• Cais da Ribeira (p49)
• Casa do Leão (p52)
• Doca Peixe (p56)
• Eleven (p55)
• Agua e Sal (p57)

stray too far from the classics you're in safe hands – try the tiramisu for dessert.
☎ 213 425 931 ✉ Travessa Poco da Cidade 60 ⏲ 12.30-2.30pm & 8-11pm Tue-Fri & Sun, 8-11pm Sat Ⓜ Baixa-Chiado 🚋 28

Cervejaria Trindade (6, B3)
Portuguese €€
A typical 19th-century *cervejaria* (beer hall), this one is a must with its groovy colourful *azulejos* (tiles) and feverish atmosphere. Drop in for anything from a quick beer to a steak-and-fries dinner, but get there early – it's usually packed every night.
☎ 213 423 506 ✉ Rua Nova da Trindade 20 ⏲ noon-1.30am Ⓜ Baixa-Chiado 🚋 28

Fidalgo (6, A3)
Portuguese €€
This tiny, welcoming restaurant buzzes with conversation at night as patrons get more

acquainted with the first-rate wine list. The restaurant has some interesting specialities, such as *medalhões de javali* (wild-boar medallions), as well as the obligatory *bacalhau* dishes.
☎ 213 422 900 ✉ Rua da Barroca 27 ⏲ noon-3pm & 7-11pm Mon-Sat Ⓜ Baixa-Chiado 🚋 28

Flores (6, A4)
Fusion €€
Situated on the ground floor of the excellent new Bairro Alto Hotel (p69), this small restaurant is one of Lisbon's best new eateries. Chef Leonor Manita comes with excellent credentials and it shows in the light seasonal menu that travels the globe without turning the food into a mish-mash of flavours. Great service and a good short wine list.
☎ 213 473 616 ✉ Praça Luís de Camões 8 ⏲ 12.30-3pm & 7.30-10.30pm Thu-Sat, until 11.30pm Ⓜ Baixa-Chiado 🚋 28

Olivier (6, A2)
Mediterranean €€€
This cosy, bottle-lined restaurant is renowned for its range of hot and cold starters on the degustation menu – which everyone orders. The crab guacamole on corn tortilla and the octopus carpaccio are so good they render the main course an anticlimax. However, great wines suggested by the knowledgeable staff will help soften the blow. ☎ 213 421 024 ✉ Rua do Teixeira 35 🕙 7.30-11pm Mon-Sat Ⓜ Baixa-Chiado 🚋 28

Pap' Açorda (6, A3)
Portuguese €€€
It's ironic that Lisbon's hipsters clamour to score a table at the eatery named after the humble stomach-filling dish, *açorda* (bread soup; see p55), but actually it's best to stick to the less-adventurous dishes here. While you should book ahead, perhaps the best part of the experience is checking out the scene from the bar while you wait. ☎ 213 464 811 ✉ Rua da Atalaia 57 🕙 12.30-2.30pm & 8.30-11.30pm Tue-Sat Ⓜ Baixa-Chiado 🚋 28

Stravaganza (6, A3)
Italian €€
This is a great late-night choice for Bairro Alto dining, with its two rooms perpetually packed with punters either using the excellent pizzas to soak up the alcohol of a Bairro bar-crawl or preparing for the hours ahead. There's a good selection of salad starters and the seafood pastas are excellent. ☎ 213 468 868 ✉ Rua do Grémio Lusitano 18-26 🕙 noon-2am Ⓜ Baixa-Chiado 🚋 28

Tavars Rico (6, A3)
French €€€€
Lisbon's oldest restaurant is a wonderfully ornate affair with delightfully old-school cooking, a comprehensive wine list and outstanding service. Seasonal game, foie gras and lobster feature heavily and there's a degustation menu if you just want to sit back and take in the ambience. ☎ 213 421 112 ✉ Rua Misericórdia 35-37 🕙 12.30-2.30pm & 8-11pm Tue-Fri, 8-11pm Sat Ⓜ Baixa-Chiado 🚋 28

ALFAMA & GRAÇA

Bica do Sapato (2, D3)
Modern Portuguese €€€€
Even after several years Bica do Sapato is still Lisbon's hottest place to dine. While we love the ever-changing photographic panels and groovy chairs, the off-hand staff are far less endearing, and while the food is artfully presented, quality rarely matches the hype. There's a sushi bar and 'caféteria' as well, but you get the distinct impression that these are sideshows to the main event, for what its worth. ☎ 218 810 320 ✉ Avenida Infante Dom Henrique, Armazém B, Cais da Pedra, Santa Apolónia 🕙 restaurant 8-11.30pm Mon, 12.30-2.30pm & 8-11.30pm Tue-Sat; sushi bar 7.30pm-1am Mon-Sat; caféteria 5pm-1am Mon, noon-1am Tue-Sat, 🚌 9, 28, 46, 59

Casa do Leão (4, A1)
Portuguese €€€
Restaurants located within the confines of tourist attractions are usually average, at best. However, this lovely restaurant at

Book ahead for the popular Pap' Acorda

Bacalhau a Bras – shredded dried and salted cod, with fried potatoes and scrambled eggs

the Castelo de São Jorge breaks the mould. During the warmer months the patio seating is prime real estate and the food, while mostly traditional fare, is great quality and skilfully cooked. Try the beef with three-pepper sauce or the *bacalhau* cooked in a corn-bread crust.
☎ 218 875 962 ✉ Rua Castelo de São Jorge, Castelo ☼ 12.30-3.30pm & 8-10.30pm 🚌 15

Casanova (2, D3)
Italian €€€
This fun, busy Italian restaurant, brought to you by the Casa Nostra (p51) crew is a more casual affair, with shared tables, no bookings and an amusing method of attracting waiter's attention (by turning on red bulbs above the tables). Pizzas are the star attraction thanks to the wood-fired oven and the place makes a great pre-Lux (p65) eatery.
☎ 218 877 532 ✉ Cais da Pedra á Bica do Sapato, Santa Apolónia ☼ 12.30-2am Wed-Sun, 7pm-2am Tue 🚌 9, 28, 46, 59

Hua Ta Li (4, A3)
Chinese €€
Visitors who have reached *bacalhau* overload (it usually takes a few days) keep this place busy ordering up any-thing except cod – and it's all satisfying stuff. The service is fast, the food is fresh, and despite it feeling incongruous eating Chinese in Alfama, we never feel guilty afterwards.
☎ 218 879 170 ✉ Rua dos Bacalhoeiros 109 ☼ noon-3.30pm & 6.30-11pm
Ⓜ Baixa-Chiado 🚌 28, 15

Jardim do Marisco (4, B3)
Seafood €€€
While there are plenty of waterfront restaurants along the Tejo, this one's consist-ently good and close to the downtown area. Weather permitting, there's no finer place to enjoy some white wine and oysters than their terrace. They do a seem-ingly bottomless *açorda de gambas* (bread soup with prawns) and fresh crusta-ceans are a popular choice.
☎ 218 824 242
✉ Avenida Infante Dom Henrique 21, Doca do Jardim do Tabaco, Pavilion A/B

☼ 1pm-midnight 🚌 9, 28, 36, 46, 59, 91

Malmequer Bemmequer (4, B2)
Portuguese €
While this place clearly gets its fair share of tourists due to its position, Malmequer remains unfazed, sending out plate after plate of simple but delicious dishes cooked on a charcoal grill. Chicken and whatever fresh fish are on offer make a good choice here.
☎ 213 421 024 ✉ Rua de São Miguel 23-5 ☼ 7-11pm Tue, noon-3pm & 7-11pm Wed-Sun 🚌 28

Restô (4, A2)
International €€
With a perch-like position overlooking Alfama, this is a wonderful Lisbon setting – good at lunch, great at dinner. While the menu was oddly assembled by colour when we visited, the food was light and perfectly matched the feeling of float-ing above the city.
☎ 218 867 334
✉ Rua Costa do Castelo 1-7 ☼ noon-3pm & 7.30pm-midnight 🚌 28

RATO, LIBERDADE, MARQUÊS DE POMBAL & SALDANHA

Ad Lib (6, A1)
Mediterranean €€€
While there are a myriad of hotel restaurants along this strip, Ad Lib stands out by offering quality cooking in stylish surroundings. The shredded codfish salad entree is a highlight and either the meat or fish mains will prove a great choice. The short wine list includes some decent half-bottles.
☎ 213 228 300 ⊠ Sofitel Lisboa, Avenida da Liberdade ⏲ 12.30-3pm & 7.30-10.30pm Ⓜ Avenida

Casa da Comida (5, C3)
Portuguese €€€
This is one of Lisbon's most enduring refined restaurants, and with good reason. In the elegant and romantic setting (adjoining a lovely patio), the emphasis at Comida is on quality Portuguese produce and measured cooking. Try the delicious shellfish soup and other great hearty

favourites such as roast kid with herbs.
☎ 213 428 295 ⊠ Travessa das Amoreiras 1 ⏲ 1-3pm & 8-11pm Mon-Fri, 8-11pm Sat Ⓜ Rato

Cervejaria Ribadouro (5, E3)
Seafood €€
With an entrance flanked by matching lobster tanks, this popular beer hall has a very obvious emphasis on seafood. The modern, brightly lit dining room buzzes with locals who come here to treat themselves to plates of fresh shellfish and the occasional steak.
☎ 213 549 411 ⊠ Rua do Salitre 2 ⏲ noon-3pm & 7.30pm-midnight Ⓜ Avenida

Comida de Santo (5, D4)
Brazilian €€€
This small, bright eatery festooned with huge tropical murals puts you in the mood for a *caipirinha* as soon as you sit down. The food is hearty Brazilian fare, with the almost obligatory *feijoada* being the dish of choice.
☎ 213 963 339 ⊠ Calçada Engenheiro Miguel Pais 39 ⏲ 12.30-3pm & 7.30pm-1am Ⓜ Rato

Consenso (5, D4)
International €€€
Located on the ground floor of the former house of the Marquês de Pombal, Consenso has been dishing up modern Portuguese and European cuisine for over 10 years. Choose from three themed areas to dine in: earth, fire or water (we like earth; air is a bar) and enjoy dishes such as *mussels à la marinière* (steamed mussels with wine and herbs) in captivating surroundings.
☎ 213 468 611 ⊠ Rua Academia das Ciências 1A ⏲ 1-3pm & 7.30-11.30pm Mon-Thu, 1-3pm & 7.30pm-12.30am Fri, 7.30pm-12.30am Sat 🚌 28 Ⓥ

Conventual (5, D4)
Portuguese €€€
Located on pretty Praça das Flores, this quaint restaurant filled with religious bric-a-brac has long been a mainstay of quality, traditional Portuguese cooking for years. While the guests are high-powered (Parliament is nearby), the service is relaxed and friendly. Stews and cod are the picks, but also great is the duck

Murals and *caipirinhas* (cocktails) at Comida de Santo

AÇORDA

Portuguese cooks have always made a little go a long way. No dish demonstrates this better than *açorda*, the bread soup that is a fixture on traditional Lisboan restaurant menus. While it can be delicious, it's little more than stale bread, onions, garlic, tomato and olive oil. Enriching the mix of broth and bread with fresh seafood (*açorda de mariscos*, usually with prawns, mussels and baby clams), for example, takes this humble dish to a new dimension. And it's amazingly filling, which was the point of the frugal exercise in the first place.

with champagne and red peppers.
☎ 213 909 196 ✉ Praça das Flores 45 ⏲ 12.30-3.30pm & 7.30-11.30pm Mon-Fri, 7.30-11.30pm Sat Ⓜ Rato

Eleven (5, C1)

Modern Mediterranean €€€€
This welcome newcomer sits atop Parque Eduardo VII, affording fantastic views right down to El Tejo from the groovy glass-fronted dining room. Eleven's stylish interior is a delight and the menu by accomplished chef Joachim Koerper is delicious and innovative, with several tasty fixed menu choices (with matching wines) alongside the à la carte offerings.
☎ 213 473 616 ✉ Rua Marquês de Fronteira ⏲ 12.30-3pm & 7.30pm-

Enoteca Charfariz do Vinho

11pm Tue-Sat Ⓜ São Sebastião, Marquês de Pombal

Enoteca Chafariz do Vinho (5, E4)

Modern Portuguese €€
Housed in a historic building of Lisbon's aqueduct system, this is an amazing setting for an *enoteca* (wine bar). There are some wonderful Portuguese wines on offer, but if you can't decide, just order a degustation menu with matching wines. Popular with kissing couples who take up the tables in the alcoves of this extraordinary structure.
☎ 213 422 079 ✉ Rua da Mãe d'Agua ⏲ 6pm-2am Tue-Sun Ⓜ Avenida

Galeto (2, D2)

Portuguese €€
The décor of this Lisbon institution comes as quite a shock to first-time visitors confronted by the time-warped perfection of its 1960s dark-wood diner-like ambience. Almost a rite of passage for post-clubbing chow, the long banquettes of the snack area are the best place to sit and order up burgers and toasted sandwiches.
☎ 213 544 444 ✉ Avenida da República 14 ⏲ 7.30-3.30am Ⓜ Saldanha

LA Caffé (5, E3)

Italian €€€
Upstairs from the Lanidor boutique is this modish restaurant, café and bar that makes a great spot to drop in even if you're not looking for a meal. However, it's worth timing your visit for a light lunch or more substantial dinner as the food is good, fresh Italian-based fare.
☎ 213 256 736 ✉ Avenida da Liberdade 129B ⏲ 9am-11pm Mon-Fri, to midnight Sat; restaurant 12.30-3.30pm & 8-11pm Mon-Fri, to midnight Sat Ⓜ Avenida Ⓥ

Luca (5, E2)

Italian €€
This modern Italian restaurant packs in local businesspeople for lunch, and those in the know come by at dinner. There is lovely organic (Portuguese) olive oil on every table, and pastas are made fresh. The seafood risotto is a (very generous) highlight. Desserts are extremely irresistible and there's Lavazza coffee for a great post-meal pick-me-up.
☎ 213 150 212 ✉ Rua de Santa Marta 35 ⏲ noon-3pm & 8-11pm Mon-Thu, noon-3pm & 8pm-midnight Fri, 8pm-midnight Sat Ⓜ Marquês de Pombal Ⓥ

O Fumeiro (6, A1)
Portuguese €€
Faithful to the cooking of the Beira Alta region of Portugal, this restaurant is about the use of smoked meats (the name means 'smokehouse'), as can be judged by the sausage-lined interior. Rustic and hearty, the food is heavy going and best when combined with copious amounts of *tinto* (red wine).
☎ 213 474 203 ✉ Rua da Conceição da Glória ◷ noon-4pm & 7pm-midnight Ⓜ Avenida

Os Tibetanos (5, D3)
Vegetarian €
In a meat-loving city where 'vegetarian restaurant' is almost a contradiction in terms, Os Tibetanos, part of a Tibetan Buddhism school, is a welcome sight for vegetarians. While lacto-vegetarians

will note that there's plenty of cheese on the menu, strict vegetarians will not fare as well. Still, who can resist a Tibetan restaurant that serves Guinness?
☎ 213 142 038 ✉ Rua do Salitre 117 ◷ noon-2pm & 7.30-9.30pm Mon-Fri Ⓜ Avenida

Terra Restaurante Natural (5, D4)
Vegetarian €
Terra (Earth) is a great vegetarian option that serves up mostly organically grown produce. The menu is eclectic (to say the least!) and while it's buffet-style, it's quite good. There's indoor or outdoor seating, some organic wines and homemade ice cream.
☎ 213 421 407 ✉ Rua da Palmeira 15 ◷ noon-3pm & 7.30-10.30pm Mon-Sat Ⓜ Rato

VEGETARIAN ANYONE?

Strict vegetarians are probably going to find Lisbon pretty hard-going as meat dishes are the staple of Portuguese cooking. Compounding this dilemma is that many dishes not containing meat will almost inevitably use a meat-derived stock or animal fat at some stage of preparation – even some desserts! Look for the restaurants listed with a Ⓥ symbol for the best options. It's better news for pesco-vegetarians – fish is fresh and fabulous – and lacto-ovo-vegetarians can try some excellent cheeses.

DOCAS, ALCÂNTARA & BELÉM

Alcântara Café (3, A2)
Portuguese €€€
Looking like a Gotham City interpretation of a Parisian brasserie, this buzzy restaurant's mix of steel, red velvet and leather is spellbinding. The service is excellent and the food a hearty mix of Portuguese classics and brasserie staples. If you're coming by the place as a pre-clubbing fuel stop, be prepared to stay longer than you planned – it's an enigmatic space.
☎ 213 637 176 ✉ Rua Maria Luísa Holstein (Primeira Rua Particula) 15 ◷ 8pm-1am, bar to 2am ⊕ 15

Caseiro (2, A3)
Portuguese €€
While the restaurants on Rua Vieira Portuense (behind Rua de Belém) facing the park make a tempting option for lunch (you could try O Carvoeiro at No 66-68), this simple place is full of locals because the food is markedly better. The fish- and meat-heavy menu is unashamedly traditional, and uncomplicated dishes such as the fried sardines are a delight.
☎ 213 638 803 ✉ Rua de Belém 35 ◷ noon-3pm & 7-10pm Mon-Sat ⊕ 15 ⊕ 27, 28

Doca Peixe (3, A3)
Seafood €€€
This is easily our favourite restaurant at this dockside area, with its lovely outdoor seating (perfect in summer) and decent, fresh seafood on

Spellbinding mix of steel, red velvet and leather: the impressive Alcântara Café (p56)

display as you walk in. Oysters on the half shell or a fish soup make for good starters and choosing fresh fish is the best option for a main course.
☎ 213 973 565 ✉ Doca de Santo Amaro, Armazém 14 ⌚ noon-3pm & 9.30pm-1am Tue-Sun 🚊 28

Restaurant Valle Flôr
(2, B3)
Portuguese €€€€
If you're not lucky enough to be holed up at the Pestana Palace (p69), this restaurant at the hotel makes for a worthwhile excursion for a romantic dinner. It's a wonderfully elegant old-world restaurant, making it hard to concentrate on the menu of classic Portuguese dishes. The service is as refined as the cuisine.
☎ 213 615 600 ✉ Pestana Palace, Rua Jaú 54 ⌚ 12.30-3pm & 8.30-10.30pm 🚊 15 🚊 27, 42, 56

Ristorant Hotel Cipriani
(3, C2)
Italian €€€€
While you battle with diplomats and the occasional

celebrity to secure a table here, this elegant restaurant at the Lapa Palace (p69) is one of the most satisfying in Lisbon. The garden views are lovely; the Italian classics on the menu are sublime and the service is undoubtedly first rate. Try the roasted scallops and follow up with lobster ravioli.
☎ 213 949 434 ✉ Lapa Palace Hotel, Rua do Pau de Bandeira 4 ⌚ 12.30-3pm & 7.30-10.30pm 🚊 28 🚊 27 **V**

PARQUE DAS NAÇÕES

Agua e Sal (2, F3)
Mediterranean & South American €€
While the Parque das Nações area is not often notable for its restaurants, thankfully this capable restaurant bucks the trend. The light, bright room offers views over to Ponte de Vasco da Gama and the food travels significantly further, with Agua e Sal's own version of salad niçoise (innovatively

replacing tuna with fresh sardines), great hearty risottos and Brazilian steaks.
☎ 218 936 189 ✉ Esplanada D. Carlos 1, Oceanário de Lisboa, Parque das Nações ⌚ noon-4pm & 8pm-midnight **M** Oriente

República da Cerveja
(2, F3)
Eclectic €€€
Beer and beefsteak are what the friendly waterfront República da Cerveja does best. Perfect for a visit either before or after Oceanário de Lisboa (p19), it does offer some seafood, such as baked cod, but the real stars of the show are the different cuts of steaks. Order your cut with one of the accompanying mouthwatering sauces, such as gorgonzola or oyster. The hardest part is choosing which beer you want from the extensive list.
☎ 218 922 590 ✉ Passeio das Tagides Pav SS-04, Parque das Nações ⌚ 12.30pm-1am Sun-Wed, 12.30pm-4am Thu-Sat **M** Oriente

Entertainment

Lisbon has an entertainment scene that can literally keep you busy 24/7. From the Art Deco cafés to the hippest clubs via dinner, *fado* and bar-hopping, it's a city that belies its conservative nature when it comes to letting its hair down. If you're here to do the sights as well as hit the nightlife, Lisbon is the most fun endurance event you can take on. Just remember to take siesta between 7pm and 9pm!

A day in Lisbon would not be complete without hanging out in one of its historic cafés, either outdoors in the sun (try Café A Brasileira, p59) or inside checking out the décor (like at Café Nicola, p59). Late afternoons are fantastic for a drink to toast the sunset (see the boxed text, p60); however, it's at night that Lisbon's entertainment scene comes alive. There are several excellent venues to take in classical concerts, dance, theatre, opera, frequent live bands and, of course, *fado*.

If you're only in Lisbon for a few days, combine *fado* with dinner (try Senhor Vinho; p61) but if you have more time it's better to bar-hop *fado*. After dinner, (around 11.30pm), head to the cobblestone, atmospheric streets of the Bairro Alto for Lisbon's famed bar scene. Arrive after 1am (especially on weekends and all summer!) and you probably won't get to see the inside of a bar, because of the crowds filling the streets outside. Just grab a takeaway *caipirinha* and join in.

Clubs in Lisbon are spread out across the centre of the city. At Santa Apolónia there's the must-do club of the scene, Lux (p65), and clubs are dotted from here down to Ponte 25 de Abril . Most clubs open at midnight so it's best to make your way down from the Bairro Alto around 2am, and head home after dawn!

LISTINGS & BOOKINGS

For details of events, grab a copy of the monthly *Follow Me Lisboa* (free) from a *turismo*. The free monthly *Agenda Cultural Lisboa* (www.lisboacultural.pt in Portuguese) includes details of the performances and screenings. Cinema listings can be found in the daily *Diário de Notícias*. Tickets are available from **ABEP Ticket Agency** (6, B2; ☎ 213 475 824; Praça dos Restauradores), Fnac (p41) and **Ticket Line** (☎ 210 036 300; www.ticketline.pt in Portuguese).

Gilded elegance: Café A Brasileira (p59)

SPECIAL EVENTS

January–February
Festival das Músicas e dos Portos (Harbour & Music Festival) Held in early February, this features *fado* paired with the traditional music from another port city, such as Athens.

March
Lisbon Arte (www.lisboarte.com in Portuguese) From mid-March to the end of April, studios all over Lisbon show contemporary art.

April
Festa da Música Centro Cultural de Belém hosts plenty of classical-music concerts.

May
Super Bock Super Rock (www .superbock.pt in Portuguese) Lisbon's biggest international rock event held over several days.

Encontros de Música Contemporânea (Contemporary Music Encounters) One of several annual international music festivals organised by the Fundação Calouste Gulbenkian (p65).

Festival Cantigas do Maio (Songs of May) The south-bank town of Seixal hosts this festival in late May, with traditional international music.

Festival Internacional de Cinema de Tróia (www.festroia.pt) Long-established, and taking place from late May to early June.

June
Festas dos Santos Populares (Festivals of the Popular Saints) Lisbon really lets its hair down. The climax of three weeks of partying, Festas de Lisboa, is celebrated with particular intensity in Alfama and Madragoa. The highlight is the Marchas Populares on the evening of 12 June when dozens of communities march along Avenida da Liberdade as part of the Festa de Santo António (St Anthony; 12 to 13 June).
Festa de São João (St John; 23 to 24 June)
Festa de São Pedro (St Peter; 28 to 29 June)

July
Jazz on a Summer's Day In the first fortnight of July, jazz lovers head to Cascais' Palmela Park Auditorium for a series of jazz concerts featuring local and international artists.

August
Jazz em Agosto (Jazz in August) Early August sees another music festival at the Fundação Calouste Gulbenkian (p65).

Festival dos Oceanos (Oceans Festival) For two weeks from mid-August, big shows and parades, concerts and gastronomic fairs all have a nautical theme.

September
Festival de Cinema Gay e Lésbico (Gay & Lesbian Film Festival; www.lisbonfilm fest.org in Portuguese) Two weeks in late September.

November
Festival Internacional de Dança Contemporânea Dance fans flock to Centro Cultural de Belém's (p65) alternative event.

CAFÉS

Café A Brasileira (6, B4) Few visitors pass up the chance to sit outdoors alongside the statue of Fernando Pessoa (the great Portuguese poet), but indoors, this legendary café's gorgeous gilded mirrors and dark wood offer superior ambience. Perfect for a late snack.
☎ 213 469 547
✉ Rua Garrett 120, Chiado
☽ 8am-2am Ⓜ Baixa-Chiado 🚃 28

Café Nicola (6, B3) While we prefer sitting outdoors at Casa Suiça, inside this historic café is a wonderfully restored Art Deco delight. While the service is haphazard, the coffee's decent.
☎ 213 460 579 ✉ Praça Dom Pedro IV (Rossio) 24, Rossio ☽ 8am-10pm Mon-Fri, 9am-10pm Sat, 10am-7pm Sun Ⓜ Rossio

Historic Café Nicola (p59)

Casa Suiça (6, C3)

This long-established favourite's outdoor terrace has a superb outlook over the *praça* (town square) and makes for an excellent spot for an afternoon beer. Inside, you're hit with the great smell of coffee and sweets, both recommended.
☎ 213 214 090 ✉ enter via Praça Dom Pedro IV (Rossio) 96-101 or Praça da Figueira ☼ 7am-9pm M Rossio

Pão de Canela (5, D4)

This great little café is set adjacent to tiny, tranquil, Praça das Flores – a tiny green spot on any Lisbon city map. The outdoor seating is prime position on weekends and it's a relaxing spot, off the tourist trail, to have a coffee and something sweet.
☎ 213 972 220 ✉ Praça das Flores 7, Príncipe Real ☼ 7.30am-8pm M Rato

Pastéis de Belém (2, A3)

It's worth a trip to Belém (p11) just for the heavenly *pastéis de belém* (custard tarts) served up at this wonderfully atmospheric tiled café on the main street. The recipe of the tart is a secret, but who cares, as long as they don't change it.
☎ 213 637 423 ✉ Rua de Belém 84-92, Belém ☼ 8am-11pm Mon-Sat, 8am-10pm Sun ☎ 15 ☎ 27, 28 ☎ Belém (Cascais line)

Pasteleria Versailles (2, C2)

This grand old *pastelaria* (pastry and cake shop) is worth a visit for the interior alone – it's wonderfully ornate, with chandeliers, wooden display cabinets and elderly ladies who can probably recall when the place was new. Great spot for coffee, cake and people-watching.
☎ 213 546 340 ✉ Avenida da República 15A, Saldanha ☼ 7.30am-10pm M Saldanha

FADO

A Baiuca (4, B2)

A friendly little place hosting *fado vadio* (open *fado*), which on a good night makes most other *fado* joints seem awfully staged. Here there's simple, unpretentious food with a lively atmosphere that gets better as the wine flows and the night wears on.
☎ 218 867 284 ✉ Rua de São Miguel 20, Alfama ☼ 8pm-midnight ☎ 28

Adega do Ribatejo (6, A3)

A fine *fado* club, where the singing and playing is never less than good and often excellent. The food's not bad either and it's hard not to like a place where the cook comes out and belts out a few tunes.
☎ 213 468 343 ✉ Rua Diário de Notícias 23, Bairro Alto € minimum spend €15 ☼ 8.30pm-12.30am Mon-Sat M Baixa-Chiado ☎ 28

Adega Machado (6, A3)

This long-standing club has stood the test of time and

SUNSET SIP

Many of Lisbon's *miradouros* (vantage points) conveniently have café-kiosks where you can sit with a nice cold beer and watch the light change. Our favourites are Alfama's **Largo das Portas do Sol** (4, B2), Bairro Alto's **Miradouro de Santa Catarina** (5, D5) and Graça's **Miradouro da Graça** (4, B1).

FINDING FADO

Taking in a *fado* performance is a 'must-do' for visitors to Lisbon. These operatic folk songs about love, death and longing can be enthralling – witnessed in the right atmosphere. And this is the conundrum of Lisbon's *fado* scene. Most venues cater mainly to tourists, so while the show is professional, it's sometimes soulless. If you visit a *fado vadio* (open *fado*) place, anyone can perform, which is either terrific or traumatic. However, if you're wandering Alfama or the Bairro Alto very late at night and hear the strains of a *fadista* giving her all, it might be an impromptu performance in a small restaurant packed with locals. You've found the 'real *fado*'.

manages to keep a credible atmosphere despite accommodating tour groups. As well as *fado,* there's folk dancing and singing performances.

☎ 213 224 640 ⊠ Rua do Norte 91, Bairro Alto € minimum spend €16 ⏱ 8.30pm-3am Tue-Sun Ⓜ Baixa-Chiado 🚃 28

Clube de Fado (4, A2)

While tour groups often make up much of the audience, the quality of the *fado* on show here is beyond question. In a lovely arched, colonnaded hall, there's decent food and it's one place where you're guaranteed a professional show every night.

☎ 218 852 704 ⊠ Rua de São João da Praça 92-4, Alfama € minimum spend €10 ⏱ 7pm-2am Mon-Sat 🚃 28

Parreirinha de Alfama (4, B2)

This local favourite attracts a knowing audience that often appears to be mesmerised by the quality *fadistas* (*fado* singers), making for a fascinating evening. The food here is also fine and the atmosphere, when it's a good night, is pretty unbeatable.

☎ 218 868 209 ⊠ Beco do Espírito Santo 1, Alfama € minimum spend €15 ⏱ 8pm-3am

Senhor Vinho (5, C5)

This renowned *fado* club is *the* place to enjoy great food and consistently good *fadistas*. While it's a small room, its reputation looms large and the idea that a new singer here could be a future *fado* star adds to the drama.

☎ 213 972 681 ⊠ Rua do Meio á Lapa, Lapa

€ minimum spend €15 ⏱ 8pm-2am

BARS

A Bicaense (6, A4)

Being located just off the Elevador da Bica, it's probably just as well the *elevador* (funicular) has stopped by the time this hip bar gets cranked up on weekends. It's worth visiting when there's a live gig – they rarely disappoint.

⊠ Rua da Bica de Duarte Beló 42A, Bairro Alto ⏱ 7pm-2am Tue-Sat Ⓜ Baixa-Chiado 🚃 28

Bar do Rio (6, A6)

Intimate, funky and on its lonesome at Cais do Sodré, this is worth hitting for a drink before heading to Lux (p65). Get there too late and it might seem like too much of an effort if it's crowded, but the staff are friendly and relaxed. Good soul/funk/house.

☎ 213 470 970 ✉ Cais do Sodré Armazém A Porta 7, Cais do Sodré ✆ 11.30-4.30am Thu-Sat Ⓜ Cais do Sodré

British Bar (6, A5)
A step back in time (literally, the bar features a backward clock), this bar resembles a turn-of-the-20th-century railway bar, right down to the suitably solemn clientele. Order an aperitif or two, though, and you'll soon make some friends.

☎ 213 422 367 ✉ Rua Bernardino Costa 52, Cais do Sodré ✆ 8am-midnight Mon-Thu, 8am-2am Fri & Sat Ⓜ Cais do Sodré

Capela (6, A3)
A former chapel now devoted to slightly off-kilter electronica and occasional house, it's good to hit early (before midnight) to appreciate the excellent DJs and before it gets maddeningly crowded. Staff keep their cool, even when the place is packed after 2am.

☎ 213 470 072 ✉ Rua da Atalaia 45, Bairro Alto, Bairro Alto ✆ 10pm-4am Ⓜ Baixa-Chiado 🚋 28

Clube da Esquina (6, A3)
A current favourite with a young, 'up for it' crowd, it's easy to spot on weekends, when groups of *caipirinha*-sipping groups spill out across the street. If you can manage to squeeze in, the décor's pretty groovy and the DJs cross over between hip-hop, electronica and house.

☎ 213 427 149 ✉ Rua da Barroca 30, Bairro Alto

✆ 10pm-4am Ⓜ Baixa-Chiado 🚋 28

Heróis (6, B3)
This café-bar is a good one to hit for an early drink on your way to the Bairro Alto. Join those reclining on the groovy furniture – the mixed crowd sipping cocktails while listening to decent laid-back house.

☎ 213 420 077 ✉ Calçada do Sacramento 14, Chiado ✆ noon-5pm Mon, noon-5pm & 8pm-12.30am Tue-Sun Ⓜ Baixa-Chiado 🚋 28

Majong (6, A3)
Another of the Bairro Alto's obligatory bars, this one attracts a bohemian bunch. It's a cool place to hang out, but on weekend nights it's too busy for all except the most determined party people.

☎ Rua da Atalaia 3-5, Bairro Alto ✆ 9pm-4.30am Ⓜ Baixa-Chiado 🚋 28

O'Gilins (6, A5)
This was Lisbon's first Irish pub and it still serves the best draught Guinness. Expect homesick expats here and live music on the

CHERRY BOMBED

Near Largo de São Domingos there are several hole-in-the-wall bars serving up little, medicinal sized shots of *ginjinha*, a cherry brandy that packs a potent punch. The most popular spot for a shot is **A Ginjinha**, (6, C2; Largo de São Domingos 8; ✆ 7am-midnight), a bar that's been inebriating locals and visitors since around 1840. You can take your medicine *com* (with) or *sem* (without) whole cherries, but really, most people find cough syrup more appealing. Try it once.

No ordinary bar — Pavilhão Chines

weekends — that's more a warning than a recommendation. Nearby **Hennessy's** (6, A5; ☎ 213 431 064; Rua Cais do Sodré 32-38) is also worth a try.

☎ 213 421 899 ✉ Rua dos Remolares 8-10, Cais do Sodré ☼ 11am-2am Ⓜ Cais do Sodré

Op Art Café (3, A3)
Highly recommended for those long summer party nights, this combo bar-club-restaurant plays some pretty decent music. The guys from Sonic (www.soniculture .com) host on Saturday nights and there are guest DJs who take you right through to dawn.

☎ 213 956 787 ✉ Doca de Santo Amaro ☼ noon-4am Tue-Thu, noon-6am Fri-Sat 🚌 15

Pavilhão Chines (5, E4)
After being greeted by a waistcoated waiter apparently hired from a different era, you soon realise that this is no ordinary bar. There are fabulous kitsch knick-knacks in cabinets, on the walls and anywhere else there's a spare piece of real estate. Locals head straight

to the back bar, as visitors get sideways on the lethal cocktails.

☎ 213 424 729 ✉ Rua Dom Pedro V 89-91, Príncipe Real ☼ 6pm-2am Mon-Sat, 9pm-2am Sun 🚋 Elevador da Gloria

Portas Largas (6, A3)
A cornerstone of the Bairro Alto drinking scene for over 10 years, it's at its best when punters, straight and gay, spill out onto the pavement nursing a pre-Frágil (p64) *caipirinha*.

✉ Rua da Atalaia 103-5, Bairro Alto ☼ 9pm-2am Ⓜ Baixa-Chiado 🚋 28

Solar do Vinho do Porto (6, A2)
Want to know just *how* seriously the Portuguese take their fortified tipple? Take a visit to this mix of tasting room, bar and temple to port, and settle into a comfy chair. Then, sample upwards of 200 different ports — preferably not in the one sitting.

☎ 213 475 707 ✉ Rua de São Pedro de Alcântara 45, Bairro Alto ☼ 11am-midnight Mon-Sat Ⓜ Baixa-Chiado 🚋 28

CLUBS

A Lontra (5, C4)
This African-themed nightclub plays a more eclectic mix of music than the others, with the mainly African-Portuguese clientele bumping and grinding to R&B, hip-hop and house. Like most of Lisbon's best clubs it fills up at about 3am.

☎ 213 956 968 ✉ Rua de São Bento 155, São Bento ☼ midnight-6am Tue-Sun Ⓜ Rato

Blues Café (3, C2)
This longstanding, popular bar-restaurant-club offers up deep-south ambience, Cajun food and 30-something mating rituals. Weeknights the bar serves up decent drinks, and on weekends the disco serves up a mix of Latin, dance-floor hits and cringe-worthy '80s throwbacks.

☎ 213 957 085 ✉ Rua Cintura do Porto 226, Doca de Alcantara ☼ 8.30pm-3.30am Mon-Thu, 8.30pm-5am Fri & Sat 🚋 15 🚌 28

Dock's Club (3, C2)
Attracting a similarly loyal crowd to the Blues Café, this mirror-ball flaunting

joint sees a well-heeled set let their hair down to everything from '80s pop and rock to the latest benign dance-floor hits.
☎ 213 950 856 ⊠ Rua Cintura do Porto, Doca de Alcantara ⏰ 11pm-6am Mon-Sat 🚋 15 🚌 28

Frágil (6, A3)
While clubbing attention has drifted down to the water, the godfather of Lisbon's nightclubbing scene still gets punters in, although mainly on weekends. A small club by today's standards, it gets pretty sweaty as a mixed crowd dances to the predominant house music. You can check the DJ roster on the website.
☎ 213 469 578 🖳 www .fragil.com ⊠ Rua da Atalaia 126, Bairro Alto ⏰ 11.30pm-4am Tue-Sat Ⓜ Baixa-Chiado 🚋 28

Incógnito (5, D5)
Bridging the two cultures of 'Bairro Alto casual' and 'Docas clubbing', this great spot plays indie, hip-hop and everything

The best club in Lisbon – Lux (p65)

in between. It's a casual place, with little attitude, and you can actually hold a conversation in the upstairs bar.
☎ 213 908 755 ⊠ Rua Poiais de São Bento 37, São Bento ⏰ 11pm-4am Wed-Sat 🚋 28

Jamaica (6, A5)
As you'd expect, there's plenty of reggae on the turntables, but they also play old favourites from almost every genre. It works because the mixed (all ages, all persuasions) crowd is up for it. Need even more reggae? Noite De Reggae (on Tuesday) is for you, though

the neighbourhood feels a bit seedy early in the week.
☎ 213 421 859 ⊠ Rua Nova do Carvalho 6-8, Cais do Sodré ⏰ 11pm-4am Mon-Thu, 11pm-6am Fri & Sat Ⓜ Cais do Sodré

Kapital (5, C6)
Kapital has witnessed thousands of young, wealthy Lisboetas quietly perspiring under their 'going out' clothes as they approach the velvet ropes of this venerable club. After getting the nod from the style police, it's a bit of a let down. The club is stylish; the ground-floor music pumps, the bar

GAY & LESBIAN LISBON

All venues listed are near the Príncipe Real (which sees its share of cruising). Note that you ring the bell for admission to most venues. Mixed crowd places include **Frágil** (above), the bar opposite it, **Portas Largas** (p63), **Heróis** (p62) and **Lux** (p65). Check out www.portugalgay.pt for more listings.

Bar Água No Bico (5, D4; Rua de São Marçal 170, Príncipe Real) An unpretentious place for a drink.

Bar 106 (5, D4; Rua de São Marçal 106, Príncipe Real) Modish spot for a drink with a dash of leather. Great on weekends.

Bric-a-Bar (5, D4; Rua Cecilio de Sousa 82-84) Cruisy legend of Lisbon's scene.

Finalmente (5, D4; Rua da Palmeira 38) Fun place with a nightly drag show at 1am.

Memorial (5, D3; Rua Gustavo Matos Sequeira 42A) Stalwart of Lisbon's Sapphic scene.

SS Bar (5, D4; Calçada do Patriarcal 38) Popular bar opposite Príncipe Real.

Trumps (5, D4; Rua da Imprensa Nacional 104B) Two bars, a sizable dance floor and legendary status.

upstairs is fine, but it's all a little reserved.

☎ 213 957 101 ✉ Avenida 24 de Julho 68, Santos ☼ 11pm-6am Tue-Sat 🚃 15 🚌 28

Kremlin (5, C6)

Lisbon's home of house doesn't really heat up until around 3am and these days Kremlin's generally only packed on weekends, with upwardly mobile Lisboetas keen to dance at this legendary club. While it's now a far cry from the heady days of the Summer of Love in '88, Kremlin can still transcend.

☎ 213 525 867 ✉ Rua Escadinhas da Praia 5, Santos ☼ midnight-4am Wed-Thu, midnight-9.30am Fri & Sat 🚃 15 🚌 28

Loft (5, D6)

Currently one of the hottest clubs for younger Lisboetas, this is a surprisingly (and thankfully) unpretentious club. While the mix of mirror balls and boys and girls in revealing tank tops is at first a little incongruous, it seems to work well – just don't get there too late as the crowd outside is massive on weekends.

☎ 213 964 841 ✉ Rua do Instituto Industrial 6, Doca de Santo Amaro ☼ midnight-4am Wed-Thu, midnight-9.30am Fri & Sat 🚃 15 🚌 28

Luanda (3, A2)

This large African club (Luanda is the capital of former Portuguese colony, Angola) is still Lisbon's favourite booty shaker. Things get hot and sweaty around 3am,

when everyone hits the floor for Luandan *kuduro* (that's Angolan-Portuguese techno), Brazilian or R&B music. Try **Mussulo** (5, E1 ☎ 213 556 872; Rua Sousa Martins 5D, Estefânia) as well, if you like the sound of Luanda.

☎ 213 624 459 ✉ Travessa Teixeira Júnior 6, Doca de Santo Amaro ☼ midnight-4am Wed-Thu, midnight-9.30am Fri & Sat 🚃 15

Lux (2, D3)

Lux is the only club in Lisbon that understands that the best clubs attract (and let in!) a diverse range of punters – which is why it's the best club in Lisbon. While you'll certainly witness a door policy at 4am on a Saturday morning, it's far more relaxed than the retro-cool surroundings would suggest. There are two dance floors, plenty of interesting art and furniture and a chilled-out terrace over El Tejo.

☎ 218 820 890 ✉ Avenida Infante Dom Henrique, Amazem A, Cais da Pedra a Santa Apolonia, Santa Apolónia ☼ 10pm-6am Tue-Sat 🚌 9, 28, 46, 59

LIVE MUSIC

Centro Cultural de Belém (2, A3)

This excellent cultural centre hosts a full programme of dance, music and theatre. Any programme that can feature artists as diverse as Mercury Rev and Woody Allen (playing with his jazz band) a couple of days apart is certainly eclectic!

☎ 213 612 400 🖳 www .ccb.pt ✉ Praça do Império, Belém 🚃 15 🚌 27, 28 🚆 Belém (Cascais line)

Coliseu dos Recreios (6, B1)

Dating from 1890, this venue has hosted just about every type of concert event you could imagine. From Miss Saigon to indie-pop darlings Sigur Rós, it's nothing if not versatile. There's a box office at the venue.

☎ 213 240 580 🖳 www .coliseulisboa.com in Portuguese ✉ Rua das Portas de Santo Antão 92, Restauradores Ⓜ Restauradores, Rossio

Fundação Calouste Gulbenkian (2, C1)

This foundation's wonderful programme is filled with

One of Europe's oldest: Hot Clube de Portugal (p66)

Rococo interior of Teatro Nacional de São Carlos (p67)

performances by their own orchestra and choir as well as frequent international guests. The orchestra programmes are notable. There's a box office at the museum (p13).
☎ 217 823 000 🖳 www .gulbenkian.pt ✉ Avenida de Berna 45a, São Sebastião Ⓜ São Sebastião

Hot Clube de Portugal
(6, A1)
A great venue for jazz aficionados, this is the real deal – one of the oldest jazz clubs in Europe. It's a tight fit on a good night but the jazz is the best in Lisbon.
☎ 213 467 369 🖳 www .hcp.pt in Portuguese ✉ Praça da Alegria 39, Restauradores 🕐 10pm-2am Tue-Sat, shows at 11pm & 12.30am Ⓜ Avenida

Paradise Garage (3, B2)
Perhaps a tad too eclectic for its own good, hosting gothic stalwarts The Mission one night and 'Ladies Night' the next, without batting an eyelid. Still, it's an excellent mid-sized venue and during summer usually hosts after-hours sessions.
☎ 217 904 080 🖳 www .paradisegarage.com ✉ Rua João Oliveira Miguens 38-48, Alcântara 🚊 15

Pavilhão Atlântico (2, F2)
A cross between a giant spaceship and an above-ground bomb shelter, this cavernous venue is where international acts usually play when they visit Lisbon.
☎ 218 918 409 🖳 www .atlantico-multiusos.pt ✉ Rossio dos Olivais, Parque das Nações Ⓜ Oriente

CINEMAS

Centro Comercial Colombo (2, B1)
There are 10 screens playing the latest ho-hum Holly-wood films at this complex, which does have good facilities.
☎ 217 113 200 ✉ Avenida Luisada, Benfica Ⓜ Colégio Militar/Luz

Complexo Amoreiras
(5, B2)
For the latest movie blockbusters (usually in the original language with Portuguese subtitles), try this multiplex.
☎ 213 878 752 ✉ Avenida Engenheiro Duarte Pacheco, Amoreiras Ⓜ Rato 🚌 58

Instituto da Cinemateca Portuguesa (5, D3)
This cinema shows art-house, world and popular film classics, with screenings from 3.30pm until 10pm. Check programming details on the website.
☎ 213 596 200 🖳 www .cinemateca.pt ✉ Rua Barata Salgueiro 39, Marquês de Pombal Ⓜ Marquês de Pombal

LISBON ON YOUR LONESOME
Lisbon is a very social place and once the *caipirinhas* start flowing in the Bairro Alto, you will soon make friends. Try **Portas Largas** (p63) or, for old-style pub atmosphere, **O'Gilins** (p62). Clubbing is a bit trickier – if you're male. If you haven't managed to hook up with a group of people, try hitting the clubs a bit earlier (around 1am), as you'll find it easier to get in.

THEATRE, DANCE & COMEDY

Chapitô (4, A2)
Those who fear clowns or dis-like street theatre should give Chapitô a wide berth – unless visiting its restaurant, Restô (p53), with the spectacular views. Companhia do Chapitô, of the theatre school, puts on performances here and there's live jazz at NetJAZZCafé.
☎ 218 855 550
🖳 www.chapito.org

✉ Costa do Castelo 1-7, Castelo 🚋 28

Teatro Nacional de São Carlos (6, B4)
Opera, ballet, theatre and orchestral performances (look for performances by the Orquestra Sinfónica Portugues) are held in this richly deco-rated theatre. The box office is open from 1pm until 7pm.
☎ 213 253 045 🖳 www .saocarlos.pt in Portuguese
✉ Rua Serpa Pinto 9,

Chiado Ⓜ Baixa-Chiado 🚋 28

Teatro São Luis (6, B4)
After a lovely renovation, the theatre now plays host to everything from Shakespeare to world-music performances. The box office is open from 1pm to 7pm Tuesday to Sunday.
☎ 213 257 650
✉ Rua Antonio Maria Cardosa 54, Chiado
Ⓜ Baixa-Chiado

SPECTATOR SPORTS

Football
Of Portugal's 'big three' clubs, two, SL Benfica (Sport Lisboa e Benfica) and Sporting (Sporting Club de Portugal), are based in Lisbon. The season runs from September to mid-June, with most matches on Sunday; check the papers (especially *Bola*, the daily football paper) or ask at ICEP (p89). Tickets cost between €20 and €50, and are sold at the stadium on match day or, for higher prices, at the ABEP ticket agency (p58).

Two of the 'big three' clubs are from Lisbon

Bullfighting
Lisbon's **Praça de Touros** (2, C1; Avenida da República), near Campo Pequeno metro, is currently closed for long-term renovation. Given the state of the site (and the snail's pace of Lisboan construction), we're not holding our collective breaths that there'll be any bullfights at this handsome bullring anytime soon. Generally the season runs from May to October, with fights usually on Thursday or Sunday.

MAJOR SPORTING VENUES
Estádio da Luz (2, B1; ☎ 217 219 540; www.slbenfica.pt; Colégio Militar-Luz metro station) SL Benfica plays at this 65,000-seat stadium, the largest in the country.
Estádio Nacional (☎ 214 197 212; Cruz Quebrada; train from Cais do Sodré) Hosts the national Taça de Portugal (Portugal Cup) each May as well as athletic events.
Pavilhão Atlântico (p66) Indoor sporting events (such as basketball) are held here in Parque das Nações.
Estádio José de Alvalade (☎ 217 516 000; Campo Grande metro station) This 54,000-seat stadium is home to Sporting (www.sporting.pt).

Sleeping

Lisbon has something approaching a decent spread of accommodation to suit all tastes and budgets, but of course it's still vital to book well ahead for summer. Off-season, however, you can usually easily find something to suit you, often at reduced rates, with a couple of days' notice. Turismo de Lisboa (p89), both at the airport and in the city, will make hotel bookings, but only for approved hotels.

Pensões (guesthouses or *pensions*) are plentiful in Lisbon and these days many of them offer great views or atmospheric locations. However, summer visitors should take note that not all of

ROOM RATES

These categories indicate the cost per night of a standard double room in high season, including taxes and breakfast.

Deluxe	from €250
Top End	€150-250
Midrange	€70-160
Budget	under €70

these places have airconditioning, which can make them a little uncomfortable at the height of summer. Midrange accommodation has a reasonably wide spread of locations and facilities, and generally offers better breakfasts than the bread, jam and bad coffee of the budget accommodation. A variety of experience awaits you in the range of top-end hotels in Lisbon; all you have to do is choose your preferred environment and atmosphere, from the Art Deco style of the Hotel Britânia (p70) to the charm of Solar do Castelo (p71). While these options do tend to be clustered along Avenida da Liberdade, this area is only a short walk or quick metro away from Rua Augusta and all the downtown action. The deluxe category offers some great palatial digs like Lapa Palace Hotel (p69), and chic newcomers such as the Bairro Alto Hotel (p69). The level of facilities in all price ranges is generally the same as that in any major European city. Unless indicated in the review, all the accommodations recommended here have Internet access.

Luxury digs: lap pool and spa at the Four Seasons Hotel Ritz Lisboa (p69)

DELUXE

Bairro Alto Hotel (6, A4)
This very welcome new-
comer offers the fantastic
mix of an elegant 19th-
century building refurbished
with modish style in the
heart of the Bairro Alto, opposite Praça Luís de Camões.
It's an intimate hotel with
just 55 rooms and outstanding personalised service.
Its restaurant, Flores (p51),
serves up excellent contemporary fare, and don't miss
the view from the rooftop
terrace.
☎ 213 408 288
🖳 www.bairroaltohotel
.com ✉ Praça Luís de
Camões 8, Bairro Alto
Ⓜ Baixa-Chiado ✂

**Four Seasons Hotel Ritz
Lisboa** (5, C2)
Recent improvements to this
hotel (such as the gorgeous
lap pool and spa) have kept
it at the top of the luxury-
digs category. All of the
usual Four Seasons ameni-
ties abound as does fantastic
artwork and sublime service
at every turn. While its
restaurant Varanda is worth
a visit, the uninspired
location of the hotel can get
tiresome.
☎ 213 811 400 🖳 www
.fourseasons.com ✉ Rua
Rodrigo da Fonseca 88,
Marquês de Pombal
Ⓜ Marquês de Pombal
✂ ✂ ✉ ♿ ♨

Lapa Palace Hotel (3, C2)
This elegant, historic hotel
embraces its hillside location
with many rooms offering
dazzling views down to Rio
Tejo. Palace Wing (part of
the original palace) rooms

are the ones to snag for
old-school charm, and dining
at Cipriani (p57) means you
don't have to hail a taxi
home. The garden pool and
spa also make the hotel hard
to leave.
☎ 213 949 494 🖳 www
.lapapalace.com ✉ Rua
do Pau de Bandeira
4, Lapa 🚊 28 🚍 27
✂ ✉ ♿ ♨

Palácio Belmonte (4, A2)
Once you actually find this
discrete gem near the Castelo
São Jorge, all that announces
it is a small plaque. This
painstakingly restored and
distinctive *palácio* (palace)
has less than a dozen
individually decorated rooms.
Fantastic views, a stylish pool
area and the notion that not
even the taxi drivers know
where it is just adds to the
unique experience.
☎ 218 816 600 🖳 www
.palaciobelmonte.com
✉ Páteo Dom Fradique
14, Alfama 🚊 28
✂ ✂ ✉ ♨

Pestana Palace (2, B3)
This wonderfully restored,
bright-yellow 19th-century
palace is a favourite of
those looking for a romantic
escape in Lisbon. While it's a
little out of the way, this hotel's not about sightseeing:
it's about good food — Valle
Flôr (p57) is one of Lisbon's
best restaurants. Relaxing
by the pool and soaking up
sun, plus the grand ambi-
ence, is best accessed from
one of the hotel's opulent
suites.
☎ 213 615 600 🖳 www
.pestana.com ✉ Rua Jaú 54,
Ajuda 🚊 15 🚍 27,42,56
✂ ✂ ✉ ♿ ♨

Pestana Palace

TOP END

As Janelas Verdes (5, B6)
This charming 18th-century
palace is located adjacent
to the Museu Nacional de
Arte Antiga (p15), and its
art connections run deep.
Famous Portuguese novelist
Eça de Queirós is said to have
lived here, with the house
being inspiration for his
novel *Os Maias*. The rooms
are a decent size, service is
friendly and the library has a
lovely terrace.
☎ 213 968 143 🖳 www
.heritage.pt ✉ Rua das
Janelas Verdes 47, Lapa
🚍 27 ✂ ✂ ♿ ♨

Hotel Altis (5, D3)
While this hotel does a
roaring business trade with
its extensive meeting and
conference facilities, its
position makes it a good
leisure option as well. There
are excellent amenities (such
as the pool, gym and sauna)
and the hotel's modern style
is unobjectionable. Its restaurant, Grill Dom Fernando, has
expansive views.
☎ 213 106 000 🖳 www
.altishotels.com in Portuguese

✉ Rua Castilho 11, Liberdade Ⓜ Avenida ✗ ✗ ⌨ ♿ ⛲

Hotel Britânia (5, E3)

This beautifully restored hotel is located in a 1940s building designed by famous Portuguese architect Cassiano Branco and has some fabulous Art Deco–style features. The service is equally old-fashioned, and coupled with the hotel's location, on a quiet street just off Avenida da Liberdade, makes for a relaxing stay. Rooms are spacious and there are all mod cons such as wi-fi.

☎ 213 155 016 ⌨ www .heritage.pt ✉ Rua Rodrigues Sampaio 17, Liberdade Ⓜ Marquês de Pombal, Avenida ✗ ✗ ♿ ⛲

Hotel Lisboa Plaza (5, E3)

Located just behind Avenida da Liberdade, this four-star offers décor courtesy of well-known interior designer Graça Viterbo, and great service. Rooms vary in size (ask for a large one) and the buffet breakfast is one of the best in town.

☎ 213 218 218 ⌨ www .heritage.pt ✉ Rua Travessa do Salitre 7, Liberdade Ⓜ Avenida ✗ ✗ ♿ ⛲

Hotel Metrópole (6, B3)

Housed above historic Café Nicola (p59), this hotel has an unbeatable position and plenty of (slightly faded) charm. Built in 1917, the hotel has period furnishings in its spacious rooms and offer views over Baixa, Alfama and to the Castelo. No Internet access.

☎ 213 219 030 ⌨ www .almeidahotels.com ✉ Praça Dom Pedro IV (Rossio) 30, Rossio Ⓜ Rossio ✗ ♿ ⛲

Hotel Tivoli Lisboa (5, E3)

While the waistcoated doormen might suggest a certain stuffiness (and if this was Paris that would certainly be true), this five-star is notable for its efficient, friendly service. Rua Augusta is an easy walk away, rooms are comfortable, the breakfast is notable and the pool packed in summer.

☎ 213 198 900 ⌨ www .tivolihotels.com ✉ Avenida da Liberdade 185, Liberdade Ⓜ Avenida ✗ ✗ ⌨ ♿ ⛲

Lisboa Regency Chiado (6, B4)

Located in the restored Armazéns do Chiado (p42) building, this stylish hotel has the best location in Lisbon. The sleek, airy rooms offer wonderful splashes of colour and booking a superior (or better) room affords fantastic views – highly recommended. Also recommended is getting back by for sunset for a drink at the bar – with even better views.

☎ 213 256 100 ⌨ www .regency-hotels-resorts.com ✉ Rua Nova do Almada 114, Chiado Ⓜ Baixa-Chiado 🚃 28 ✗ ✗ ♿ ⛲

Sofitel Lisboa (6, A1)

This modishly renovated Sofitel is now an exceptional choice for those who crave a brand-name hotel in Lisbon. It's also one of the best positioned of these hotels, with Rua Augusta just a short stroll away. The rooms, with all new features, are a delight, and the hotel's bar and Ad Lib restaurant (p54) are worth visiting.

☎ 213 228 300 ⌨ www .sofitel.com ✉ Avenida Da Liberdade 127, Liberdade Ⓜ Avenida ✗ ✗ ♿ ⛲

ROOM WITH A VIEW

Lisbon's romantic streets are matched by equally dreamy views and several of Lisbon's hotels have fantastic vistas. Here's a selection of the best:

- Olissipo Castelo (p72)
- Pensão Ninho das Águias (p73)
- Lisboa Regency Chiado (right)
- Lapa Palace Hotel (p69)
- VIP Eden (p72)

Castle comfort: Solar do Castelo Hotel, located within the walls of Castelo de São Jorge

Solar do Castelo (4, A1)
Located within the outer walls of the Castelo de São Jorge, this historic building of the 18th century is a charming hotel. Rooms are positioned around a lovely inner courtyard and garden, and the whole place keeps the medieval feel while infusing contemporary touches, making it a very romantic and distinctive hotel.
☎ 218 806 050 ▭ www.heritage.pt ✉ Rua das Cozinhas 2, Castelo 🚇 28 ✗ 🔀 ♿

MIDRANGE

Albergaria Senhora do Monte (2, D2)
Near the Miradouro da Senhora do Monte – which translates to some of the most breathtaking views in Lisbon – this hotel is quite a lovely retreat. The rooms are simple but comfortable and to make the most of the location, book a room with one of the huge terraces. No Internet access.
☎ 218 866 002 ▭ senhoradomonte@hotmail.com ✉ Calçada do Monte 39, Graça 🚇 28 🔀 ♨

Dom Carlos Liberty (5, E2)
This completely refurbished hotel is a contemporary, stylish affair that's a short metro hop or walk down to the Baixa. Rooms have a low-key tan-and-white colour scheme and the bathrooms are freshly decorated and well stocked.
☎ 213 173 570 ▭ www.domcarlosliberty.com ✉ Rua Alexandre Herculano 13, Marquês de Pombal Ⓜ Marquês de Pombal ✗ 🔀 ♿ ♨

Hotel Jorge V (5, D3)
This comfortable little hotel, just off Avenida Da Liberdade, is starting to show its age, but private balconies, a decent breakfast (for a three-star) and friendly staff make it a decent option in this price range.
☎ 213 562 525 ▭ www.hoteljorgev.com ✉ Rua Mouzinho da Silveira 3, Marquês de Pombal Ⓜ Avenida, Marquês de Pombal ✗ 🔀 ♿ ♨

Hotel Lisboa Tejo (6, C3)
This adventurously designed hotel is one of the most distinctive in Lisbon. The

achingly hip touches of the public areas, however, don't extend to the rooms, which also (particularly on the lower floors) can be noisy. Occasional queues for breakfast and an irregularly staffed bar don't help matters, but its fantastic location and design makes it a difficult hotel to leave out – so we didn't.
☎ 218 866 182 ▭ www.evidenciahoteis.com ✉ Poço do Borratém 4, Rossio Ⓜ Rossio ✗ 🔀 🚐 ♿ ♨

Hotel Miraparque (5, D1)
This traditional three-star overlooks Parque Eduardo VII (upper floors have better views) and while quite a restrained property, it's a fine base for a Lisbon stay with Baixa-Chiado only a couple of metro stops away.
☎ 213 524 286 ▭ www.miraparque.com ✉ Avenida Sidónio Pais 12, Marquês de Pombal Ⓜ Marquês de Pombal ✗ 🔀 ♿ ♨

Hotel NH Liberdade (5, E3)
This chic little hotel is often overlooked due to its location in an upmarket little shopping

mall. Stylish and spare, it's hard to believe that it's several years old. The rooms are modern, comfortable and come with all mod cons (including wi-fi) and there's a rooftop bar and swimming pool – perfect for a summer visit.

☎ 213 514 060 🖳 www .nh-hotels.com ✉ Avenida da Liberdade 180B, Liberdade Ⓜ Avenida
✄ ✂ ☕ ♿ ♨

Hotel Veneza (5, E3)
While the rooms couldn't possibly match the foyer and staircase for grandeur, it's probably just as well as they are just a little over the top. The rooms themselves are mid-sized, modest and quite comfortable and the staff accommodating. No Internet access.

☎ 213 522 618
🖳 www.3khoteis.pt
✉ Avenida da Liberdade 189, Liberdade
Ⓜ Avenida ✂

Olissipo Castelo (4, A1)
Spectacular Lisbon views are really the selling point of this surprisingly modern hotel. While the decoration is nondescript, the vistas certainly keep most guests happy, with the 2nd- and 3rd-floor rooms (with balconies) offering the best views. For sightseeing you'll be hopping on and off the No 28 tram an awful lot – no great hardship there, however!

☎ 218 820 190 🖳 www .olissipohotels.com ✉ Rua Casa do Castelo 112-126, Castelo 🚋 28 ✄ ✂ ♨

VIP Eden (6, B2)
While this 'aparthotel' has fairly anonymously styled studios (for up to two people)

LUSCIOUS LISBON DESIGN
Until the last couple of years Lisbon had a dearth of decently designed digs. However, today Lisbon has some amazing properties – and we're not talking the kind of tired minimalism that signifies 'design' hotels – these have oodles of character. Here's the best of them:

- Palácio Belmonte (p69)
- Solar dos Mouros (below)
- Hotel Lisboa Tejo (p71)
- York House (below)
- Solar do Castelo (p71)

and apartments (for up to four people), thankfully the gorgeous Art Deco façade of this former cinema complex remains intact. The rooms are well-equipped and convenient for long stays, but the big selling points are the location and the extraordinary views from the rooftop, which has a bar and a pool.

☎ 213 216 600 🖳 www .viphotels.com ✉ Praça dos Restauradores 24, Restauradores Ⓜ Restauradores
✄ ✂ ☕ ♿ ♨

Solar dos Mouros (4, A2)
This small hotel's eight rooms are eclectic and stylishly decorated, with wonderfully abstract paintings (mainly by owner-painter Luís Lemos). The rooms offer either river or castle views from its wonderful vantage point and this, along with

personal service and decent breakfasts, makes it a romantic choice for art lovers. No Internet access.

☎ 218 854 940 🖳 www .solardosmouros.pt ✉ Rua do Milagre de Santo António 4, Alfama 🚋 28 ✂

York House (5, B6)
A wonderful little oasis hidden away among greenery, this former 17th-century convent has oodles of charm in its modern and classically decorated rooms. The hotel restaurant serves up delicious dishes and the seating spills into its sun-dappled courtyard, the perfect place for catching up on some reading – a relaxing retreat.

☎ 213 962 435 🖳 www .yorkhouselisboa.com
✉ Rua das Janelas Verdes 32, Lapa 🚋 15 🚌 27
✄ ✂ ☕ ♿ ♨

WORK, PLEASURE OR LEISURE

Here's our list of the best hotels to suit your needs:

- Business trip – Hotel Tivoli Lisboa (p70)
- Romantic sojourn – Lapa Palace Hotel (p69)
- Location, location, location – Lisboa Regency Chiado (p70)
- Old-school charm – Pestana Palace (p69)

BUDGET

Hotel Astoria (5, D2)

While the pretty façade of Hotel Astoria makes promises that the rooms and offhand service don't even come close to keeping, this is still a clean and reliable choice, only a couple of metro stops from Baixa-Chiado. The rooms are simple but spotlessly clean and always include decent linen. Breakfast, while rudimentary, is always fresh. No Internet access.

☎ 213 861 317 🖳 www .evidenciahoteis.com ✉ Rua Braamcamp 15, Marquês de Pombal Ⓜ Marquês de Pombal ✖

Pensão Londres (6, A2)

We thoroughly recommend booking early to score the rooms with views on the higher floors of this unpretentious, simple little *pension*. They're the best-value rooms with a view in town, and also give you great access to the Bairro Alto nightlife. There are rooms with or without bathroom. No Internet access.

☎ 213 462 203 🖳 www .pensaolondres.com.pt ✉ Rua Dom Pedro V 53, Bairro Alto Ⓜ Baixa-Chiado 🚋 28 ✖

Pensão Ninho das Águias (4, A1)

Located just below the castle, the best feature of this small *pension* is the remarkable views (insist on booking one with views). The rooms are adequate, and some have shared bathrooms. No Internet access.

☎ 218 854 070 ✉ Rua Costa do Castelo 74, Castelo 🚋 28

Pensão Praça da Figueira (6, C2)

Clean, bright, well-run and with *praça* (town square) views in some of the rooms, this is a fantastic deal in this price range. The rooms are a decent size, there's a communal kitchen with fridge, and the management is friendly and helpful. No Internet access.

☎ 213 426 757 🖳 rrcoelho@clix.pt ✉ 3rd fl, Travessa Nova de São Domingos 9, Rossio Ⓜ Rossio 🚋 15 ✖

Residencial Duas Nações (6, C4)

On a corner of Baixa's pretty, pedestrianised Rua Augusta, it's surprising that this good-value 19th-century place hasn't been transformed into something altogether more grand. However, the deluxe category's loss is your gain. Make sure you get a room on the upper floors, preferably not on Rua Augusta (the accordion players on the street are tuneless). No Internet access.

☎ 213 460 710; fax 213 470 206 ✉ Rua da Vitória 41, Baixa Ⓜ Baixa-Chiado 🚋 28

Reliable Hotel Astoria

About Lisbon

HISTORY
The Phoenicians
While the Iberian peninsula had been inhabited since the Stone Age, in 1200 BC the Phoenicians established a trading post in Lisbon in order to resupply their boats en route from Canaan (Lebanon and Syria) to Cornwall, calling it Alis Ubbo (meaning 'safe harbour'). The ancient Greeks knew the city as Olissipo, a derivation of Ulysses, whom they believed founded the city. However, the Phoenicians were well established by then, intermarrying with Celts and trading with northern Lusitanian tribes.

The Romans & the Moors
The Romans decided to invade Iberia in 237 BC. After years of fighting the Lusitanians, the Romans integrated Iberia into their empire under Julius Caesar, renaming the city Felicitas Julia in 60 BC. Emperor Augustus established a period of peace (Pax Romana) and life did remain peaceful until the Visigoths invaded in AD 409. German tribes fought over Lisbon for a few hundred years until it fell to the Moors in 711, becoming part of Al-Andalus, with Cordoba its capital.

Age of Discovery
At the end of the four-month Siege of Lisbon in 1147, the Crusaders recaptured the city en route to the Holy Land, although nearly a century passed before the Christians reconquered Portugal. In the meantime, Afonso Henriques was crowned Portugal's first king in 1139 and the country was recognised in 1143, when the Treaty of Zamora brought peace between Portugal, Castille and Leon. After Afonso III moved the capital from Coimbra to Lisbon, around 1255, development was swift as trade surged, impeded temporarily by the Black Death in 1349. A showdown in 1385, between João 1's Portuguese troops and the powerful Spanish, resulted in an emphatic victory, consolidating Portugal's independence and starting its age of imperialism.

Gargoyle at Mosteiro dos Jeronimos (p10)

João's son, Prince Henry the Navigator, financed expeditions along Africa's coast, and made a fortune from slaves and gold. By the time he died in 1460 he mono polised coastal trade; however, the biggest breakthroughs were Vasco da Gama's discovery of the route to India in 1498, leading to control of Goa, the Indian Ocean and spice trade; Pedro Álvares Cabral's arrival in Brazil, opening up more trading routes; and Magellan's circumnavigation

Evidence of Portugal's sailing history adorns the streets of Lisbon

of the globe from 1519 to 1522. With merchants flocking to trade in gold, gems, spices and silk, Lisbon was the centre of global trade and a vast, prosperous empire, reflected in the exuberant Manueline architecture developed under Dom Manuel I.

Spanish Rule
The Spanish Inquisition saw the expulsion of Lisbon's Jews and their entrepreneurial expertise. Expensive maritime expeditions and the maintenance of an empire took its toll on leaders. This was compounded by Dom Sebastião's disastrous crusade to Morocco in 1557 where, in defeat, Sebastião and most of Portugal's nobility were killed. When his successor, elderly relative Cardinal Henrique, died heirless in 1580, Sebastião's uncle, Felipe of Spain, claimed the throne. Crowned king after defeating the Portuguese he began a long period of Hapsburg rule from Madrid. Not until 1640, when nationalist rebels stormed the palace, forcing the Spanish out, did the Duke of Bragança retake the throne as João IV.

Independence & Enlightenment
When Portugal declared independence from Spain in 1668, a new period of prosperity began, sparked by diamond and gold discoveries in Brazil, and stimulated by the wine trade. This wealth was squandered on extravagant building projects, which were ruined with the Great Earthquake of 1755. João V's son, Jose I, enlisted the enlightened Marquês de Pombal who grasped the opportunity to modernise. He rebuilt the city, establishing efficient government, protecting trade, reforming education and abolishing slavery.

Revolution & Republic
Following the 1807 French invasion and the royal family's exile to Brazil, Britain battled to protect Portugal's trade routes. With the royals ruling from Brazil, Portugal virtually became a Brazilian colony and British

SAY IT WITH FLOWERS – THE CARNATION REVOLUTION

The coup of 25 April 1974, which lead to regime change (from repressive dictatorship to military-backed communist government to liberal administration a couple of years later), was almost bloodless. The revolutionaries used no force. Persuaded by a carnation-waving public to proceed peacefully, the soldiers symbolically placed red carnations – an expression of love and affection – in their rifle barrels. It was a rather 'peace, love and harmony' affair all round – the secret signal used to ignite the revolt was the radio broadcast of Portugal's entry to the Eurovision Song Contest, the Paol de Carvalho song, *E depois do adeus,* while Zeca Afonso's *Grandola Vila Morena* was played to confirm the successful start to the coup. The revolution is remembered on Freedom Day, 25 April.

protectorate, and descended into political chaos. Decades of struggles between the nobility and a liberal reactionary movement led to the 1910 revolution and the declaration of a republic.

An unstable economy, squabbling political factions (45 governments in 16 years!) and a powerful military meant circumstances were ripe for the 1926 coup. António de Oliveira Salazar rose rapidly from finance minister to prime minister, a job he'd hold for 36 years. In 1933 Salazar declared a 'new state', introducing censorship, banning strikes and political parties, and establishing a repressive dictatorship. While the economy stabilised, the unpopular and expensive wars in the African colonies destabilised the military, and a revolutionary movement was born. When Salazar retired, following a stroke in 1968, the country was in chaos. A 1974 coup, dubbed the Carnation Revolution (see the boxed text, above), ushered in independence for the African colonies; however, the arrival of hundreds of thousands of *retornados* (African refugees) caused social and political turbulence.

Contemporary Lisbon

When Portugal joined the European Community (now the EU) in 1986, socialist leader Mário Saores was its first civilian president in 60 years. The stable, centre-right government lasted a record 10 years and attracted substantial EU funding. The subsequent extraordinary economic growth enabled timely public works projects, including the Ponte de Vasco da Gama and the redevelopment of a site to host Expo '98. Its ocean theme was a powerful reminder of a period when Lisbon prospered by its relationship with the sea, setting a positive tone for the new millennium.

ENVIRONMENT

Almost medieval in its appearance, Lisbon was one of the most rundown of European cities before joining the EU. Massive funding enabled improved living conditions, urban regeneration, restoration of historic neighbourhoods and redevelopment of the polluted waterfront. This included the cleanup of the 340-hectare industrial wasteland that became the Parque das Nações (Nations Park) site for Expo '98, and the creation of an 80-hectare 'green leisure zone', the Parque do Tejo e do Trancão, on the site of a landfill. Some Lisboan municipalities established innovative local environmental projects, such as Oeiras, which set up a backyard organic composting programme to reduce the amount of waste municipalities must collect, transport, treat and dispose of. While these projects

Oceanário at Parque das Nações (p19)

raised public awareness, thus increasing demands for a greener city, Lisbon's improved economy created a surge in city traffic and greater air pollution.

GOVERNMENT & POLITICS
Since 1255, when the capital moved from Coimbra, Lisbon has hosted the Unicameral Assembleia da Republica, Portugal's parliament. The 2005 election saw the Partido Socialista (PS), elected for four years, win 121 of 230 parliamentary seats, and its leader, Jose Socrates, become prime minister. Socrates leads a council of ministers, and the Assembleia da Republica approves the government's legislative programme. Head of state is the president (currently, Jorge Sampaio of the PS), elected for five-year terms. The Região de Lisboa e Vale do Tejo administers the 11,890 sq km of Lisbon region's 52 *concelhos* (municipalities), run by a mayor and assembly, the largest being Lisbon City. The current Lisbon mayor, Pedro Miguel de Santana Lopes, was prime minister before Socrates.

ECONOMY
Having been one of Europe's poorest economic performers, Portugal experienced rapid development after joining the EU. Helped by EU funding, the Partido Social-Democrata (Social Democratic Party) introduced wide reforms and privatisation. While traditional industries, such as

Palácio de São Bento (p26), host to the Portuguese Parliament

textiles, agriculture, cork and wine remained strong, tourism, finance, and manufacturing grew slowly.

Portugal's massive budget deficit violated EU public debt limits and lead to recession in 2002, compounded by competition from Eastern Europe entering the EU. As the gap between rich and poor widened, average wages remained at the lower end of the EU scale, and urban poverty increased. Lisbon now has shanty towns of the kind you expect to see in Brazil rather than Europe.

Native product, *quercus suber* (cork oak)

While the new Socialist government has introduced some austere measures to reduce the spiralling deficit, the unpopular fiscal tightening significantly affected public-sector employees, resulting in strikes and mass demonstrations. An increase in value-added tax and high oil prices has impacted the government's popularity, sorely felt at council elections in 2005. After the Paris riots triggered several copycat car burnings in Lisbon, the government pledged 25 million euros to improve social inclusion in 'problematic' suburbs.

SOCIETY & CULTURE

Portugal's 2005 population was 10.6 million, with 2.5 million living in the Lisbon region and 560,000 in the centre. Official figures put ethnic Portuguese at 95% of the population with 5% (500,000) comprising immigrants from former African colonies, Eastern Europe and China, although it's thought this 5% figure is misleading due to the immeasurable number of illegal immigrants living in depressed housing estates and shack settlements in outer Lisbon.

> **DID YOU KNOW?**
> - While over 90% of Portuguese are Roman Catholic, Islam is Portugal's second religion
> - Lisbon's population is around 564,000, while greater Lisbon has a population of over 2,500,000
> - Over 20% of foreigners legally resident in Portugal are from Cape Verde

Lisbon has experienced successive waves of immigrants since the 1960s, starting with almost a million *retornados* after its African colonies gained independence. The late '70s saw refugees arrive from war-torn Angola and Mozambique, followed by immigrants from Guinea-Bissau, São Tomé e Príncipe, Timor and Goa. Brazilians have a sizable community, while increasingly, Chinese and Eastern Europeans are moving to Lisbon, mostly working in construction, public works, manufacturing and hospitality.

While the downside has been increasing ethnic tension, racial discrimination, prostitution and drug-related crime, the media has been criticised for distorting reality, reinforcing stereotypes and sensationalising

Youngsters and their homemade shrine for the Festa de Santo Antonio in Alfama (p59)

minor incidents. Municipalities, NGOs and welfare groups have established programmes aimed at fighting social exclusion and racism, and encouraging integration.

Roman Catholicism is still the dominant faith, and the Festa de Santo António is enthusiastically celebrated in Lisbon each June. Although the Portuguese are conservative (due to Catholic influence and decades of Salazar's repression), Lisboetas are less so. While traditional dance and music are revered, Lisbon is increasingly gaining a reputation as a Portuguese Ibiza thanks largely to Lux, the Bairro Alto bar scene, and its embrace of gay culture.

While football is a national obsession here as in Spain, bullfighting is also considered to be a noble tradition, although it's less popular (and far less brutal, as the bull isn't killed during the fight) in Lisbon than it is in Madrid. Around 300 bullfights are held each year, from Easter Sunday to All Saints' Day.

ARTS
Architecture

The 1755 earthquake left little pre-18th-century architecture to admire. Some sublime survivors include the Romanesque Sé Cathedral, Italian Renaissance–style Igreja de São Vicente de Fora and Igreja de São Roque. Belém's flamboyant Manueline architecture was financed by the extravagant Dom João V from 17th-century gold and diamond discoveries in Brazil – once the gold ran out, architects returned to classicism, as exemplified by Palácio de Queluz. After the earthquake, the Marquês de Pombal rebuilt the city in a style defined by its simplicity and clarity, as seen in the Baixa. The Elevador de Santa Justa was built in 1902 by Raul Mésnier, a colleague of Gustave Eiffel. Portugal's greatest contemporary architect, Álvaro Siza Vieira, restored much of the Chiado, which had been destroyed in the 1988 fire. However, his masterpiece is the Pavilhão de Portugal, built especially for Expo '98. The Parque das Nações is home to stunning buildings designed by Peter Chermayev (Oceanário de Lisboa) and Santiago Calatrava (Gare do Oriente).

Literature

Lisbon's literature has been dominated by lyric poetry and realist fiction. The epic poem from national hero Luís Vaz de Camões, *Os Lusiadas* (The Lusiads; 1572), was about Vasco da Gama's 1497 voyage to India as much as it was about the Portuguese spirit. Nineteenth century romantic Almeida Garrett combined poetry, prose, drama and philosophy. His masterpiece is the innovative political-travelogue-cum-romance *Viagens na Minha Terra* (Travels in My Homeland; 1846). José Maria Eça de Queirós is considered to be the greatest realist writer and his *O Crime do Padre Amaro* (The Sin of Father Amaro; 1875) was made into a film in 2002. Lisbon's most brilliant writer and poet, Fernando Pessoa (1888–1935), wrote prolifically in four distinct styles, but only *Mensagem* (Message; 1934) was published during his lifetime. The country's greatest writer, José Saramago, won the 1998 Nobel Prize for Literature. Repressed during Salazar's dictatorship, he gained fame with *Memorial do Convento* (1982) and the extraordinary *Blindness* (1995).

Music

Emerging from 18th-century working-class areas like Alfama, *fado* (meaning 'fate') is a musical expression of sorrow, drowning in the uniquely Portuguese state of being, *saudade,* a longing for something lost or never gained. This melancholic music is traditionally performed by a singer, accompanied by a 12-string Portuguese *guitarra* (guitar) and a conventional guitar. Amália Rodrigues (below), is universally considered the greatest *fadista*. *Fado,* traditional folk songs, and music from Europe and Africa, all influenced *música popular,* a 1960s folk movement that developed when musicians like José Afonso joined with poets to create a new

Photographs of *fado* singers named Maria

THE QUEEN OF FADO

Amália Rodrigues was born in 1920 in Lisbon. While still a teenager she was singing in clubs and performed her first professional engagement at age 19. Quickly recognised as a major talent, she brought to *fado* her charisma and interpretive ability that is still unsurpassed in the genre. She pushed the boundaries of *fado,* using orchestral arrangements and singing the words of poets, while becoming an international star in the process. In her 40s, she pushed the boundaries again, with her (1962) album with composer Alain Oulman, which was decidedly more 'operatic' than most *fado* records up to that point. She continued to perform and record until around 1990. On 6 October 1999, Amália Rodrigues died at the age of 79 in her Lisbon home, which is now a museum, Casa Museu de Amália Rodrigues (p21).

music dealing with social and political issues. Censored under Salazar, lyrics were overtly political after 1974 and singers used performances to support revolutionary groups. Singer-songwriter Júlio Pereira has experimented with the folk roots of *música popular* while adding contemporary innovations. Carlos Paredes and António Chaínho have transformed the sounds of the Portuguese guitar along with master folk artists Brigada Victor Jara, Trovante, Almanaque and Madredeus. Also popular in Lisbon are African sounds such as the melancholic *morna* from Cape Verde, exemplified by Cesária Évora.

Painting

The most important of Portugal's early art is the altarpiece *Adoration of St Vincent,* by 15th-century painter Nuno Gonçalves, in Lisbon's Museu Nacional de Arte Antiga. Manueline artists Jorge Afonso (painter to Dom Manuel I), Cristóvão de Figueiredo, and Gregório Lopes created art remarkable for its luminous colour and sense of realism. The 17th-century female artist Josefa de Óbidos attracted attention with her rich still life paintings. Domingos António de Sequeira produced wonderful portraits in the late 18th century, while Silva Porto and Marquês de Oliveira worked in the naturalist and Romantic styles of the 19th century. While naturalism tended to dominate 20th-century art, Amadeo de Souza Cardoso worked in cubism and expressionism and Maria Helena Vieria da Silva produced abstract art. The work of Almada Negreiros, father of modern-art movement, can be seen in the Centro de Arte Moderna.

Cinema

Portugal's most prolific, innovative and acclaimed film director, Manoel de Oliveira (b 1908), shot his first documentary at age 20, his first feature at 34, and continues to make films and teach even today. His *Journey to the Beginning of the World* (1997) was Marcello Mastroianni's last film before he died, while *A Carta* (The Letter; 1999) starring Mastroianni's daughter, Chiara, won the Jury Prize at Cannes. Apart from a few controversial films by younger directors – *Ossos* (Bones; 1997) by Pedro Costa, *Os Mutantes* (The Mutants; 1999) and *Agua e Sol* (Salt & Water; 2001) by Teresa Villaverde, and Maria de Medeiros's *Capitães de Abril* (Captains of April; 2000) – it's still Oliveira who attracts the most attention. His latest, *A Talking Picture* (2004), is a travelogue starring John Malkovich, and his most extraordinary film yet.

Instituo da Cinemateca Portuguesa (p66)

Directory

ARRIVAL & DEPARTURE
Air
Lisbon is served by one international airport, Aeroporto de Lisboa (LIS), also known as Aeroporto da Portela, about 20 to 30 minutes northeast of the city centre. Portugal's international airline is TAP Air Portugal, while the main domestic airline is PGA Portugália Airlines.

In arrivals, you'll find various car-rental agencies and an office for Turismo de Lisboa (p89).

INFORMATION
General inquiries (☎ 218 413 500)
Flight information (☎ 218 413 700; www.ana-aeroportos.pt)

AIRPORT ACCESS
The **AeroBus** (🕓 7am-9pm) departs from outside the arrivals gate every 20 minutes, taking 30 minutes to get to Cais do Sodré station, stopping at Praça do Comércio. You'll need to purchase a Lisboa Card (24 hours, €13.50/6), which you can continue to use on all city buses, trams and *ascensors* (funiculars) throughout Lisbon. You can also take bus 44 from Gare do Oriente until 9.30pm.

The taxi fare for the 20-minute ride to the city centre is around €7 plus €1.50 for luggage.

Bus
There are two major transport terminals for buses arriving at and departing from Lisbon. The bus terminal at **Gare do Oriente** (2, F2; Parque das Nações) is at street level, along with shops, a post office and some car-rental offices. Bus company **ticket booths** (🕓 9am-5.30pm Mon-Thu, 9am-7pm Fri) are above the terminal on the 1st floor. For weekend trips, book by phone through the bus company, and pay on the bus. European long-distance bus travel is handled via the Spanish branch of **Eurolines** (www.eurolines.es), operating through Lisbon's

Intercentro (☎ 218 957 398). The Portuguese carrier **Eva** (☎ 289 899 700; www.eva-bus.com) also operates from here.

Arco do Cego (2, D2; ☎ 213 545 439; Avenida João Crisóstomo, Saldanha), near Saldhana metro stop, is the base for all long-distance coaches operated by **Rede Expressos** (☎ 213 103 111), which includes Rodoviária do Tejo, Belos Transportes and other smaller companies, and **Eva/Mundial Turismo** (☎ 213 147 710). The two companies service the whole country.

Train
The **Gare do Oriente** (2, F2; Parque das Nações) train terminal is on the 1st floor, where you'll find main-line train ticket booths. Nearly all services, including international ones, stop at Gare do Oriente, linked to the city centre by metro and to the airport by bus 44. The metro is on basement level, along with banks, shops, cafés, police, and a left-luggage locker room.

Santa Apolónia (4, A3; ☎ 218 884 025/26/27; 🕓 6.45am-10pm Mon-Fri, 6.45am-7.30pm Sat & Sun) train station has an international section that's open from 8am to 8pm daily with a bank, a travel agency, car-rental desks, a snack bar, ATMs and an Ask Me Lisboa kisok (p89).

There are two standard long-distance rail journeys into Portugal, taking the TGV Atlantique from Paris to Irún (in Spain), changing trains in Spain for Portugal. The daily journey from Paris to Lisbon takes about 20 hours. You can book directly with **SNCF** (French Railways; www.sncf.com). The main Spain–Portugal rail route from Madrid to Lisbon via Cáceres on the Talgo Lusitânia takes 10 hours.

Travel Documents
PASSPORT & VISA
Visitors to Lisbon should carry their passport at all times. Nationals of EU countries need no visa for any length of stay in Portugal. Those from Canada, New Zealand, USA and

Australia can stay for up to 90 days in any half-year without a visa. Everyone else needs a visa (unless they are a spouse or child of an EU citizen). General entry requirements apply to citizens of other signatories of the 1990 Schengen Convention (Austria, Belgium, Denmark, Finland, France, Germany, Greece, Iceland, Italy, Luxembourg, the Netherlands, Norway, Spain and Sweden). A visa issued by one Schengen country is valid for travel in all the others, but unless you're a citizen of the UK, Ireland or a Schengen country, you should also check visa regulations with the consulate of each Schengen country you plan to visit. You must apply for any Schengen visa in your country of residence.

To extend a visa or 90-day period of stay after arriving in Portugal, contact the **Serviço de Estrangeiros e Fronteiras** (5, D1; Foreigners Registration Service; ☎ 213 585 545; Rua São Sebastião da Pedreira 15; 🕑 9am-3pm Mon-Fri). For an extension, you'll need proof of financial independence.

Customs & Duty Free

Portugal allows visitors to bring as much currency as they like into Portugal. The duty-free allowance for travellers over 17 years old from non-EU countries is 200 cigarettes, or the equivalent in tobacco, and 1L of alcohol that has over 22% alcohol content or 2L of wine or beer. Nationals of EU countries can bring in 800 cigarettes or the equivalent in tobacco, plus alcohol not amounting to more than 10L of spirits (ie 20L of fortified wine, 60L of sparkling wine, 90L of still wine or 110L of beer). There's no more duty-free shopping in Portugal's airports.

Left Luggage

The airport does not provide a facility for left luggage. You'll find left-luggage locker rooms at Gare do Oriente on the basement level, and also at the Santa Apolónia and **Arco do Cego** (2, D2; ☎ 213 545 439; 🕑 8am-7pm Mon-Fri, 8am-1pm & 2-6pm Sat & Sun) bus terminals.

GETTING AROUND
Travel Passes

For your stay in Lisbon, we recommend that you get the **Lisboa Card** (24 hours €13.50/6, 48 hours €23/9.50, 72 hours €28/11.50), which gives you access to all public transport (including *ascensors* and trains to Sintra and Cascais), admission to museums and monuments, as well as other discounts. These cards are available at Turismo de Lisboa offices (p89).

Bus & Tram

Carris (☎ 213 613 060, 213 613 038; www .carris.pt in Portuguese) operates all buses and trams. Most run from 6am to 1am, with some later services. Individual tickets can be bought on board, although you'll find it easier to use the Lisboa Card (above).

Metro

The ever-expanding underground metro system, **Metropolitano de Lisboa** (www .metrolisboa.pt in Portuguese; 🕑 6.30am-1am), is excellent for short hops across the city, and to Gare do Oriente and Parque das Nações. Individual tickets cost €0.70 while a *caderneta* of 10 tickets costs €6.35. Tickets can be purchased from windows or automatic dispensers in metro stations. Single tickets must be validated in the machine at the platform entrance. Useful signs include *correspondência* (transfer between lines) and *saída* (exit to the street). There are also great maps to get you oriented before leaving the station.

Train

Lisbon has three major train stations. Santa Apolónia is the terminal for IC and IR trains from northern and central Portugal, and for international services; all Santa Apolónia services also run through the increasingly important Gare do Oriente. Barreiro, across the river, is the terminal for *suburbano* services to Setúbal and long-distance services to southern Portugal. Connecting ferries leave frequently from the pier at Terreiro do Paço (4, A3). At this pier, you buy both the ferry ticket and onward train ticket.

There are four smaller stations: **Cais do Sodré** (5, E6; Praça do Duque da Terceira) is the terminal for Cascais and Estoril; **Rossio** (5, E4; Praça dom Pedro IV/Rossio) serves Queluz-Belas, Cacém and Sintra; and **Entrecampos** (2, C1; Avenida 5 de Outubro) station serves the northern Azambuja line as well as Fertagus trains across the Ponte 25 de Abril. **Entrecampos Poente** (2, C1; 200m east of Entrecampos) serves the suburban line to Cacém.

Ferry

Commuter ferries cross the Rio Tejo (Tagus River) to/from Lisbon, and cross the mouth of the Rio Sado. The Transtejo ferry line has several riverfront terminals *(estações fluviais)*. From the eastern end of the **Terreiro do Paço terminal** (4, A3; off Praça do Comércio) catamarans ferry passengers the 30-minute trip across the Rio Tejo to Montijo (€1.75) and Seixal (€1.40) every hour (every 15 minutes during rush hours, less often at weekends). From the main part of the terminal, called Estação do Sul e Sueste, Soflusa ferries run every 30 to 60 minutes to Barreiro (€1.50), where you can pick up rail connections to the Alentejo and Algarve. Next door, at Cais da Alfândega, passenger ferries go every 10 minutes, all day, to Cacilhas (€1.50, 10 minutes).

Taxi

Taxis are plentiful, and good value over short distances. Ordinary taxis are usually marked A (which stands for *aluguer* – for hire) on the door, number plate or elsewhere. They use meters and are available on the street and at taxi ranks, or by telephone for a surcharge of €0.75.

Autocoope (☎ 217 932 756)
Rádio Táxis de Lisboa (☎ 218 119 000)
Teletáxis (☎ 218 111 100)

The fare on weekdays during daylight hours is about €1.90 *bandeirada* (flag fall) plus around €0.40 per kilometre, and a bit more for periods spent idling in traffic. If you think you may have been cheated by a taxi, get a receipt from the driver, note the car's registration number and your time of departure and arrival, and call the **Inspecção-Geral das Actividades Económicas** (5, C3; ☎ 213 831 523; Rua de São Bento 347) to report the incident. The police or Turismo de Lisboa (p89) should also be able to help.

Car

On a short trip to Lisbon, you're unlikely to need your own wheels, as distances are close, and parking and driving restrictions do not make driving a pleasant experience.

To rent a car in Portugal you must be at least 25 years old and have held your driving licence for over a year. Nationals of EU countries, Brazil and the USA need only their home driving licences to drive a car. Others should get an International Driving Permit (IDP) through an automobile licensing department or automobile club in their home country.

PRACTICALITIES
Business Hours

Most shops open Monday to Friday 9am to 1pm and 3pm to 7pm, Saturday until 1pm, and close on public holidays like Easter, Christmas, and New Year's Day. Malls open 10am to 10pm daily. Banks open Monday to Friday 8.30am to 3pm, post offices Monday to Friday 9am to 12.30pm and 2.30pm to 5.30pm. Government offices open 9am to noon and 2pm to 5pm Monday to Friday. Museums usually close on Monday, and generally open Tuesday to Sunday 10am to 12.30pm and 2pm to 5pm.

Climate & When to Go

Lisbon falls in both the Atlantic and Mediterranean climatic zones, thereby enjoying a pleasantly temperate climate year-round. Its mean annual temperature is 17°C, with average temperatures in winter of 13°C and

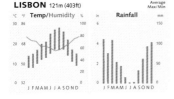

LISBON 121m (403ft)

27°C in summer. Summer temperatures reach the mid-30s, although the proximity of the Atlantic Ocean insures some cooling breezes. Most rain falls during the winter months. July and August are the hottest, driest months, while November to February is the wettest and coldest period. The high season is mid-June to mid-September.

Disabled Travellers

Alfama and Bairro Alto, with their hilly cobbled streets, are challenging for the disabled (deficientes). The Baixa's flat grid and Belém are fine, and Parque das Nações is accessible. Public offices and agencies are required to provide access and facilities for disabled people, but private businesses are not. Lisbon airport is accessible.

INFORMATION & ORGANISATIONS

Dial-a-ride Disabled Bus Service Lisbon (☎ 217 585 676) could come in handy. **Secretariado Nacional de Rehabilitação Lisbon** (☎ 217 929 500; www.snripd.pt) is the national governmental organisation representing the disabled, with information on barrier-free accommodation, transport, shops, restaurants and sights.

Discounts

The Lisboa Card (p83) allows discounts or full admission to many attractions and free travel on public transport. The **International Student Identity Card** (ISIC; www.istc.org) and **International Teacher's Identity Card** (ITIC; www.istc.org) enable holders to get discounts on everything from accommodation to museum admission fees. If you're over 65 you're eligible for discounts

on museums, sightseeing excursions and train fares (half-price on weekdays).

Electricity

Portugal uses a two-pin plug outlet (sometimes with a third, middle pin) and voltage is 220V, 50HZ.

Embassies

Australia (5, E3; ☎ 213 101 500; 2nd fl, Avenida da Liberdade 200, Liberdade; Avenida metro)

Canada (5, E3; ☎ 213 164 600; 3rd fl, Avenida da Liberdade 196, Liberdade; Avenida metro)

UK (5, C4; ☎ 213 961 191; Rua de São Bernardo 33, Estrela; tram 28, bus 9 or 27)

USA (2, C1; ☎ 217 273 300; Avenida das Forças Armadas; Jardim Zoológico metro)

Emergencies

To avoid having your bag snatched, or being targeted by pickpockets, avoid appearing like an obvious tourist, and don't flash your cash, camera or mobile phone. Keep valuables in the hotel safe.

Police, fire & ambulance (☎ 112)

Tourist police (☎ 213 421 634) 24-hour emergency service

Rape crisis hotline (☎ 800 202 148)

Fitness

One of the most popular forms of fitness in Lisbon is to go surfing at the nearby beaches. Other than that, it's football or perhaps a run at Parque Eduardo VII (p27), but not after dark. Outside the hotels, the best health clubs are in Lisbon's malls – believe it or not. Head to the Centro Vasco da Gama's **Solinca Health and Fitness Club** (2, F2; ☎ 218 930 706; 7am-10pm Mon-Fri, 9am-8pm Sat & Sun).

Gay & Lesbian Travellers

In Lisbon acceptance has increased, although Portugal is a conservative Catholic country, so homosexuality is still outside the norm. Lisbon has an excellent gay and lesbian network and nightlife (see p64). Lisbon holds Gay Pride marches, but outside these events the gay community keeps a discreet profile. When you go to a gay bar or club, you usually have to ring a doorbell for admission. **Portugal Gay** (www .portugalgay.pt/guide_uk) includes an English-Portuguese message board.

Health
IMMUNISATIONS
Travel insurance is advisable to cover any medical treatment you may require in Lisbon. No vaccinations are required for entry into Portugal, although a yellow-fever vaccination certificate is required of travellers coming from infected areas and arriving in or bound for the Azores or Madeira.

PRECAUTIONS
Lisbon tap water is safe to drink, although bottled water is very popular. Your main risks are likely to be an upset stomach from enjoying too much food and wine, or sunburn. Take care with shellfish – cooked mussels that haven't opened properly can be dangerous.

MEDICAL SERVICES
Travel insurance is advisable to cover any medical treatment you may need while in Lisbon. Citizens of EU countries are covered for medical treatment throughout the EU on presentation of a health card, though fees are likely to be charged for medications, dental work and secondary examinations. *Centros de saúde* (state-administered medical centres) are open 8am to 8pm, though you're unlikely to find any English-speakers. Hospitals with 24-hour accident and emergency departments include the following:
Hospital Britânico (5, B4; British Hospital; Hospital Inglês; ☎ 213 955 067, 213 976 329; Rua Saraiva de Carvalho 49, Estrela; tram 28, bus 9 or 27) A private hospital with English-speaking staff and doctors.
Hospital de São José (6, C1; ☎ 218 860 848; Rua José António Serrano, Anjos; Martim Moniz metro)

DENTAL SERVICES
For dental emergencies ask hotel desk staff, who generally keep a list of dental clinics with English-speaking practitioners.

PHARMACIES
Farmácias (pharmacies) in Lisbon often have English-speaking staff. They are generally open from 9am to 6pm weekdays (closing at lunch), and Saturday morning. To find an after-hours pharmacy call directory inquiries (☎ 118) or check the daily *Público* newspaper. A competent central pharmacy is **Farmácia Estácio** (6, B3; ☎ 213 211 390; Rossio 62, Rossio; Rossio metro).

Holidays
Banks, *turismos* (tourist offices), offices, department stores and most shops generally close on the following holidays:
New Year's Day 1 January
Carnaval Tuesday February/March (day before Ash Wednesday)
Good Friday & Easter Sunday March/April
Freedom Day 25 April
Labour Day 1 May (celebrating 1974 revolution)
Corpus Christi May/June (ninth Thursday after Easter)
Portugal Day 10 June
Feast of the Assumption 15 August
Republic Day 5 October
All Saints' Day 1 November
Independence Day 1 December
Feast of the Immaculate Conception 8 December
Christmas Day 25 December

Internet
Lisbon's hotels are starting to catch on that not just business travellers need the Internet and many now have broadband Internet access. Wireless-device-wielding travellers will find wi-fi in some hotels, and free wi-fi at the large shopping centres (p42) in the food courts. Internet cafés are thin on the ground in Lisbon.

INTERNET CAFÉS
CiberOceanos (2, F2; ☎ 218 951 995; Gare do Oriente; 🕙 10am-11pm; Oriente metro)

NetCentreCafe (6, A2; ☎ 213 240 012; Rua Diário de Notícias 157-159, Bairro Alto; 🕙 4pm-2am; Baixa-Chiado metro, tram 28)

Western Union (6, C2; Rossio; 🕙 9am-9.30pm Mon-Fri, 9am-7pm Sat & Sun; Rossio metro)

USEFUL WEBSITES
LonelyPlanet.com (www.lonelyplanet .com) For travel information, links, and advice from other travellers.

Portugal Tourism (www.portugal.org) Portugal's official tourism site.

Portugal's Yellow Pages (www .paginasamarelas.pt) Portugal's phone numbers at your fingertips.

Lost Property
The **tourist police** (6, B2; ☎ 213 421 634; Praça dos Restauradores; Restauradores metro) at the Palácio Foz should be your first place of call.

Metric System
Portugal uses the metric system.

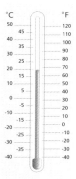

TEMPERATURE
°C = (°F - 32) ÷ 1.8
°F = (°C x 1.8) + 32

DISTANCE
1in = 2.54cm
1cm = 0.39in
1m = 3.3ft = 1.1yd
1ft = 0.3m
1km = 0.62 miles
1 mile = 1.6km

WEIGHT
1kg = 2.2lb
1lb = 0.45kg
1g = 0.04oz
1oz = 28g

VOLUME
1L = 0.26 US gallons
1 US gallon = 3.8L
1L = 0.22 imperial gallons
1 imperial gallon = 4.55L

Money
Since 1 January 2002 Portugal has used the euro. While prices jumped, the easy conversion (100 escudos equalled half a euro) made the changeover less painful than in other countries.

The most convenient way to get your money is from an ATM. Most banks have a Multibanco ATM, accepting Visa, Access, Mastercard, Cirrus and so on. Your home bank will usually charge a transaction fee. Credit cards are increasingly being accepted at most places in Lisbon, but always check at small restaurants and bars.

Banks and bureaux de change are free to set their own rates and commissions, so a low commission might mean a skewed exchange rate. There are bureaux de change at Rossio and Praça da Figueira.

Newspapers & Magazines
Foreign-language press have a significant presence – especially English-language papers in the south and Eastern European newspapers in cities, thanks to large immigrant populations. Portuguese-language dailies include *Diário de Notícias*, *Público* and *Jornal de Notícias*. The tabloid is *Correio da Manhã*. International newspapers are widely available.

Photography & Video
Portugal uses the PAL video system, incompatible with both the French Secam system and the North American and Japanese NTSC system. For accessories etc head to Fnac (p41).

Post
Post offices are called **CCT** (www.ctt.pt). Ordinary mail *(correio normal)* goes in the red letter boxes; airmail, express and priority mail *(correio azul)* go in the blue boxes. You can send post to poste restante in main post offices of cities and large towns.

The most convenient **post office** (6, B2; ☎ 213 238 700; 🕙 8am-10pm Mon-Fri, 9am-6pm Sat & Sun) in town is on Praça dos Restauradores. The **central post office** (6, C5; ⏲ 8.30am-6.30pm Mon-Fri) is on Praça do Comércio. There is a 24-hour post office at the airport.

POSTAL RATES

Stamps are available at post offices, at kiosks and shops with a red 'Correios – selos' (stamps) sign, and from vending machines. 'By air mail' is *por avião* in Portuguese; 'by surface mail' is *via superfície*. Postcards and letters up to 20g cost €0.72/0.56/0.30 outside Europe/within Europe/local. International mail *(correio azul)* costs €1.75 for a 20g letter.

Many post offices have NetPost for Internet access, but these are frequently out of order. If they do work, it costs €2.40 per hour, with cards costing €5.49.

Radio

State-owned Rádiodifusão Portuguesa (RDP) runs Antena 1, 2 and 3, with Portuguese broadcasts and evening music. For English-language radio you can tune into the BBC World Service and Voice of America (VOA).

Telephone

Public phones are increasingly operated only by phonecard. However, you can also call from booths in Portugal Telecom offices and post offices – pay when your call is finished. Calls from public phones are charged per number of *impulsos* (beeps or time units) used. The price per beep is fixed (€0.06) with a phonecard, but it's the length of time units that is the key to the cost. The duration depends on destination, time of day and type of call. Coin telephones cost €0.07 per beep; hotel and café phones rack up three to six times the charges. It costs two/three beeps extra to make a domestic/international connection. All but local calls are cheaper from 9am to 9pm weekdays, all weekend and on holidays.

PHONECARDS

The easiest way to call someone within Portugal is with a Portugal Telecom *cartão*

telefónico (phonecard). These cards are available for €3, €6 or €9 from post and telephone offices and many newsagents. A youth or student card should get you a 10% discount.

From Portugal Telecom, you can get a Hello CardPT or PT CARD Europe, both costing €5. You call an access number then key in the code on the back of the card. This is a cheaper way of making international calls. There are lots of competing cards offering much the same service. Note that peak and off-peak periods vary from company to company.

MOBILE PHONES

Portugal has one of the highest penetrations of mobile phones in the world. The phone system of Portugal is GSM and there are 3G services available. For more information on services, visit Portugal Telecom's website at www.telecom.pt.

COUNTRY & CITY CODES

To call Portugal from abroad, call the international access code ☎ 00, then Portugal's country code ☎ 351, then the number. All domestic numbers have nine digits.

USEFUL PHONE NUMBERS

Portugal's directory inquiries number is ☎ 118; operators will search by address as well as by name. The international directory inquiries operator is ☎ 177. To make a reverse-charge call *(page no destino)* with the help of a multilingual operator, dial ☎ 171.

Television

Rádio Televisão Portuguesa (RTP-1 and RTP-2), Sociedade Independente (SIC) and TV Independente (TV1) fill airtime with Portuguese and Brazilian soaps, game shows, reality shows and subtitled foreign movies. You'll find CNN or BBC World at all but the most inexpensive hotels.

Time

Portugal is on GMT/UTC in winter and GMT/UTC plus one hour in summer. This puts it an hour earlier than Spain, year-round. Clocks are set forward by an hour on the last Sunday in March and back on the last Sunday in October.

Tipping
If you're satisfied with the service, tip 5% to 10%. Bills at pricier restaurants may already include *serviço* (service charge). After a snack at a bar or café, some shrapnel is enough. People don't tend to tip taxi drivers, but they will be happy if you offer them 10%.

Toilets
Public toilets *(sanitários* or *casas de banho)* are rare, though coin-operated street toilets are increasingly common. Most people go to the nearest café for a drink or pastry and use the facilities there. Look for a 'WC' sign, or 'H' for *homens* (men) or 'S' for *senhoras* (women).

Tourist Information
Ask Me Lisboa are very useful information kiosks run by Turismo de Lisboa. The following are the most useful branches:
Belém (2, A3; Mosteiro dos Jerónimos ☽ 10am-1pm & 2-6pm Tue-Sat)
Rua Augusta (6, C4; near Rua de Conceição; ☽ 10am-1pm & 2-6pm)
Santa Apolónia (4, A3; inside train station; ☽ 8am-4pm Tue-Sat)

For national inquiries try **ICEP** (6, B2; ☎ 213 463 314; Palácio Foz, Praça dos Restauradores; ☽ 9am-8pm), the *turismo* most efficiently run by the state's tourism organisation. There's also a Turismo de Lisboa desk here. The **Lisboa Welcome Center** (6, C5; ☎ 210 312 810; Praça do Comércio; ☽ 9am-8pm) is friendly and efficient. There's a branch of **Turismo de Lisboa** (☎ 218 450 660; ☽ 8am-midnight) at arrivals at the airport, and it has maps, advice on taxis and other transport, and can make hotel reservations.

The handy and free *Follow Me Lisboa,* a twice-monthly Portuguese-English leisure guide, is available from all the offices listed above.

Women Travellers
Women travelling alone in Portugal are quite safe. However, anyone walking alone in the dimly lit areas of Lisbon at night runs the risk of being mugged.

LANGUAGE
Portuguese, along with French, Italian, Spanish and Romanian, is a Romance language closely derived from Latin. It is spoken not only in Portugal but also in Brazil and five African nations. English is the most widely spoken foreign language in Lisbon, and you'll find that many service employees (eg, in tourist offices, hotels and restaurants) can usually speak some French and German too.

Useful Words & Phrases
Hello.	*Bom dia.*
Hi.	*Olá.*
Good day.	*Bom dia.*
Good evening.	*Boa noite.*
See you later.	*Até logo.*
Goodbye.	*Adeus.*
How are you?	*Como está?*
Fine, and you?	*Tudo bem, e tu?*
I'm pleased to meet you.	*Prazer em conhecê-lo/-la.* (m/f)
Yes.	*Sim.*
No.	*Não.*
Please.	*Faz favor.*
Thank you (very much).	*(Muito) Obrigado/Obrigada.*(m/f)
You're welcome.	*De nada.*
Excuse me. (to get past)	*Com licença.*
Excuse me. (asking a question)	*Desculpe.*
What's your name?	*Como se chama?*
My name is ...	*Chamo-me ...*
Where are you from?	*De onde é?*
I'm from ...	*Sou (da/do/de) ...*

May I take a photo (of you)?	*Posso tirar-lhe uma foto?*
Do you speak English?	*Fala inglês?*
Do you understand?	*Entende?*
I (don't) understand.	*(Não) Entendo.*
Could you please ...?	*Pode por favor ...?*
repeat that	*repetir isso*
speak more slowly	*falar mais devagar*
write it down	*escrever num papel*
Who?	*Quem?*
What?	*(O) Quê?*
When?	*Quando?*
Where?	*Onde?*
Why?	*Porque?*
Which/What?	*Qual/Quais? (sg/pl)*

Getting Around

Where's ...?	*Onde fica ...?*
Can you show me (on the map)?	*Pode mostrar-me (no mapa)?*
What's the address?	*Qual é a morada?*
How far is it?	*Qual a distância daqui?*
How do I get there?	*Como é que eu chego ali?*
Turn ...	*Vire ...*
at the corner	*na esquina*
at the traffic lights	*no semáforo*
left	*à esquerda*
right	*à direita*
here	*aqui*
there	*ali*
near ...	*perto ...*
straight ahead	*em frente*
north	*norte*
south	*sul*
east	*este*
west	*oeste*

Transport

Which ... goes to Lisbon?	*Qual o ... que vai para Lisboa?*
boat	*barco*
intercity bus	*camionetes*

local bus	*autocarro*
ferry	*ferry*
plane	*avião*
train	*comboio*
When's the ... (bus)?	*Quando sai o ... (autocarro)?*
first	*primeiro*
next	*próximo*
last	*último*
A ticket to ...	*Um bilhete para ...*
Is this the (bus) to ...?	*Este (autocarro) vai para ...?*
What time does it leave?	*Que horas sai?*
What time does it get to ...?	*Que horas chega a ...?*
Do I need to change?	*Tenho de mudar de linha?*
Is this taxi available?	*Este táxi está livre?*
How much is it to ...?	*Quanto custa ir a ...?*
Please put the meter on.	*Por favor ligue o taxímetro.*
Please take me to (this address).	*Leve-me para (esta morada), por favor.*

Emergencies

Help!	*Socorro!*
It's an emergency.	*É uma emergência.*
I'm lost.	*Estou perdido/ perdida. (m/f)*
Where are the toilets?	*Onde ficam os lavabos?*
Go away!	*Vai-te embora!*
Call ...!	*Chame ...!*
a doctor	*um médico*
an ambulance	*uma ambulância*
the police	*a polícia*

Health

I'm ill.	*Estou doente.*
I need a doctor.	*Preciso de um médico.*
It hurts here.	*Aqui dói.*

I've been vomiting.	*Tenho estado a vomitar.*
(I think) I'm pregnant.	*(Acho que) Estou grávida.*
antiseptic	*antiséptico*
asthma	*asma*
contraceptives	*anticoncepcional*
diarrhoea	*diarréia*
fever	*febre*
pain	*dores*
painkillers	*analgésicos*
Where's the nearest ...?	*Onde fica ... mais perto?*
dentist	*o dentista*
doctor	*o médico*
hospital	*o hospital*
medical centre	*a clínica médica*
I feel ...	*Estou ...*
dizzy	*com tonturas*
nauseous	*com naúseas*
I'm allergic to ...	*Sou alérgico/a à ...*
antibiotics	*antibióticos*
aspirin	*aspirina*
bees	*abelhas*
peanuts	*amendoins*
penicillin	*penicilina*

Around Town

What time does ... open?	*A que horas abre ...?*
I'd like to buy ...	*Queria comprar ...*
I'm just looking.	*Estou só a olhar.*
May I look at it?	*Posso vê-lo/la?* (m/f)
How much is it?	*Quanto é?*
That's too expensive.	*É muito caro.*
I'll take it.	*Vou levar isso.*
Where is ...?	*Onde fica ...?*
an ATM	*um multibanco*
a bank	*o banco*
a bookstore	*uma livraria*

the ... embassy	*a embaixada do/da ...*
a foreign exchange office	*uma loja de - câmbio*
a laundrette	*uma lavandaria*
a market	*o mercado*
a pharmacy	*uma farmácia*
the police station	*o posto de polícia*
the post office	*o correio*
a supermarket	*o supermercado*

Numbers

0	*zero*
1	*um/uma* (m/f)
2	*dois/duas* (m/f)
3	*três*
4	*quatro*
5	*cinco*
6	*seis*
7	*sete*
8	*oito*
9	*nove*
10	*dez*
11	*onze*
12	*doze*
13	*treze*
14	*quatorze*
15	*quinze*
16	*dezesseis*
17	*dezesete*
18	*dezoito*
19	*dezenove*
20	*vinte*
21	*vinte e um*
22	*vinte e dois*
30	*trinta*
40	*quarenta*
50	*cinquenta*
60	*sessenta*
70	*setenta*
80	*oitenta*
90	*noventa*
100	*cem*
200	*duzentos*
1000	*mil*

Index

See also separate indexes for Eating (p93), Entertainment (p94), Shopping (p94), Sights with map references (p94) and Sleeping (p95).

SLEEPING

FEATURES

Bonjardim	*Eating*
Chapitô	*Entertainment*
Majong	*Drinking*
Café Nicola	*Café*
Sé Cathedral	*Highlights*
Zara	*Shopping*
Museu do Design	*Sights/Activities*
Pestana Palace	*Sleeping*

AREAS

	Building
	Land
	Mall
	Market
	Other Area
	Park/Cemetery
	Sports
	Urban

HYDROGRAPHY

	River, Creek
	Intermittent River
	Canal
	Swamp
	Water

BOUNDARIES

	State, Provincial
	International
	Ancient Wall

ROUTES

	Tollway
	Freeway
	Primary Road
	Secondary Road
	Tertiary Road
	Lane
	Under Construction
	One-Way Street
	Unsealed Road
	Mall/Steps
	Tunnel
	Walking Path
	Walking Trail/Track
	Pedestrian Overpass
	Walking Tour

TRANSPORT

	Airport, Airfield
	Bus Route
	Cycling, Bicycle Path
	Ferry
	General Transport
	Metro
	Cable-Car, Funicular
	Taxi Rank
	Tram

SYMBOLS

	Bank, ATM
	Buddhist
	Castle, Fortress
	Christian
	Diving, Snorkeling
	Embassy, Consulate
	Hospital, Clinic
	Information
	Internet Access
	Islamic
	Jewish
	Lighthouse
	Lookout
	Monument
	Mountain, Volcano
	National Park
	Parking Area
	Petrol Station
	Picnic Area
	Point of Interest
	Police Station
	Post Office
	Ruin
	Telephone
	Toilets
	Zoo, Bird Sanctuary
	Waterfall